Workplace Champion By Example

A Step-by-Step Training Guide

Growing Employee Loyalties

Secrets Every CEO Should Know

John Smithman

Advance Praise For Workplace Champion By Example

"A book I wish I had when I first became a manager and supervisor!

I found it to be a wonderful, easy to understand synthesis of 'the basics' every new or aspiring manager could use in order to set themselves for success. The many tips, analogies and examples made the material easy to digest.

For those with experience managing, this book provides a quick and delightful review from which to self-evaluate current habits, analysing and identifying possible areas for improvement!"

> Shelley Brierley, MEd, CCC, RCC, RTC
> Oasis Consulting Ltd.
> www.thecircleofstrength.com

"Wow! I wish that I'd had tools like this when I first took on a leadership role!

I love how you are able to introduce concepts and introspective ideas by asking (seemingly), simple questions. Your anecdotes are right on the money and really help drive your ideas home.

This is a fantastic tool for new organizational leaders."

> *Rabbi Don Pacht, Head of School*
> *Vancouver Hebrew Academy*

"This book fills the gap that occurs when good workers are thrust into supervisory roles without adequate training.

The book coaches workers through their new roles, showing how to build self-confidence while assessing the new environment and work flow. Its purpose is to help supervisors to become workplace champions quickly and effectively.

This book shows how to simply manage the balancing act between workers and top management. You not only get the questions... you also get the answers."

> *Raymond (Ray) J Bertrand, RAS*
> *Registered Addictions Specialist*
> *Motivational Speaker and Trainer*

Table of Contents

FIGURES

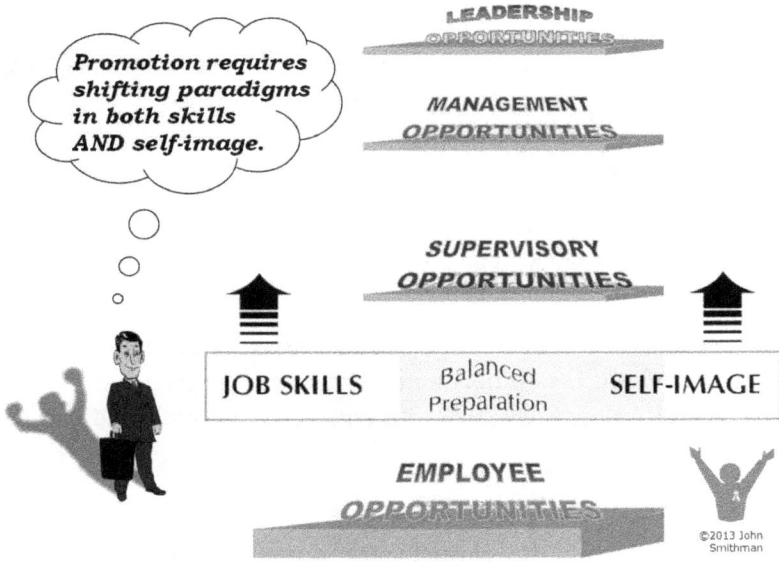

Figure 1: Workplace Champion

Preface

In 1961, my Rock'n'Roll Band The Megatones won a radio talent show contest. This was my first happy experience leading others.

Since then, I've supervised people in businesses from military to airlines, from service and retail to university administration. I've trained and coached people on every level for over 50 years.

As a coach, I've seen people become managers and leaders. I've helped groups of workers become highly-effective teams of workplace champions.

First as a manager and then as a coach, I have seen people achieve success by building their skills and self-confidence. They become productive champions when managed by competent leaders.

People don't leave companies, they leave bad bosses. This book will help you become the good boss people love to serve.

John Smithman

Introduction

Congratulations on your promotion! You're about to experience one of the most difficult, or most joyful, times of your career.

Questions and Answers

Ask yourself these 99 questions and read my answers to prepare yourself for success. The questions will help you anticipate and meet the challenges and opportunities of your new job.

The questions are split into four stages: [B]ase, [W]orkplace, [P]lans and [C]hampions. Each question number contains a letter showing the group to which it belongs (e.g., QP72 for a Planning question, and QC86 for a question on Championship.)

This book is a coaching guide for new supervisors who want:

- To make a good first impression that grows over time;

- To not only fit in, but to gradually take on a leadership role;

- To build and lead effective teams of dedicated workplace champions;

- To lead their companies into a prosperous future; and

- To become a workplace champion along the way.

Expect to take several months to complete this book. It should act as your guide to assuming more responsibility and gaining better results. Review and test your learning anytime by re-reading the companion 99 Questions workbook.

Subscribe to the Workplace Champion blog for articles and new insights into supervising or feel free to ask for help along the way: John Smithman. I'll answer your questions as quickly as I can, time permitting. If you want some dedicated personal time with me to discuss your workplace challenges, you can book my consulting time on the WorkplaceChampion.com blog site.

Good Supervisors are Undervalued

Don't underestimate the value of developmental supervision. There are no limits to the positive values that good supervisors bring to their companies. Moving from supervision to leadership, you will gradually learn how to build an effective workplace. You will convert dependent workers who must be motivated to follow orders into independent, self-motivated and self-led teams. These are the high-performance teams who learn to recognize and conquer the common challenges of today's workplaces by themselves.

Shifting Roles

To help you understand the roles of workers and bosses versus teams and team leaders, I will refer often in this guidebook to your first employees as workers. This supports their roles as people who do what they are told and no more. Later, as they grow, they will become team members. And, bosses will become leaders to help define their evolving work style.

Shifting Paradigms

Here you will find concepts based on fundamental principles of leadership and team development that have led common companies to uncommon success. Your basic thinking about management will shift, as subtle seeds of change introduce new concepts like the roles of selling strategies and consensus-building to create champions in the workplace™. Champions who motivate others while growing themselves.

Bonus!

At the back of the book are reminder lists of Insights, Quotations, Rules, and Stories from the book. At the proper time as situations unfold you'll learn to use them to help you travel smoothly along the path from supervisor to leader. The simplicity and power of these simple concepts will reveal the powerful results within your grasp.

My Mind is a Verb - Creative Thinking Frames

That the mind is easy distracted has been proven in many tests where people are invited to focus on one thing, while something else is happening unseen. I've seen experiments where gorillas, clowns or witches pass undetected among members of a busy scene.

In some respects it seems scary that we could miss something dangerous moving among us. However, think instead of the potential of such phenomena to help us.

For years, magicians have purposefully distracted us in a busy scene so they can make things appear or disappear. What if managers could use this phenomenon to their advantage? A creative thinking frame acts as a filter to engage the focusing function of our minds to see things that may not be seen normally.

Insights are creative thinking frames that enhance an event's salient features. Consider how a picture frame focuses our attention on certain complementary picture elements. Changing the frame changes our perspective on what's important. The correct frame fixes our attention on the possibilities, while the wrong one shows us the frustrations.

Look at Vincent Van Gogh's "Starry Nights" with different frames and see picture elements with colors matching the frame jump out at you, while others retreat.

Figure 2: Starry Nights framed

"My Mind is a Verb" - THE YELLOW CAR

A related phenomenon: If while talking with you today, I mention that I haven't seen any yellow cars lately. I guarantee that for the rest of the week, I'll see lots of yellow cars, because I brought them into my mind's focus. The image I plant in my mind dominates my thinking for a time. This is what **Insights** do for you.

The Basic Tools For the Job

YOUR HEAD: Your head is full of ideas of what you can do in the job. But be careful. Now is the time for questions, not statements. People will be watching you, judging you. So tread softly and be respectful. Act as a "curious detective". You are the face of Humility at this stage of your growth.

YOUR HEART: You're excited, proud, and a bit nervous. The environment is new, strange. Don't be too vulnerable. Just relax and enjoy the new experiences as they come. There will be lots of time for you to let your feelings show.

YOUR WORKING TOOLS: As you become more effective, you will gather tools to help you do your work more efficiently. But for now, arm yourself with four tools: a pen, steno pad, desktop calendar and to-do lists. These will be your toolkit.

Your steno pad will be dated and archived. It is portably light and doesn't take up much space. Its pages are wired in and should not be removed, as they record your development path as supervisor.

It will be your journal, your diary, your record of events in your life as a supervisor. You will be able to refer to previous meetings and what was agreed upon with others. It will help you recall decisions made and why they were made. When your thoughts are written down, your mind is clear to make new decisions.

Your desktop calendar should be placed on the desk you use when you talk on the phone or use a computer or other communication device. It provides a place for you to plan your days. Most calendars cover a year or 18 months; a month on each page with a box for each day of the month.

Write in the boxes such things as appointments, phone call reminders, books or equipment purchased, and so on. You'll find many other uses for your desktop calendar.

Your pen, not a pencil, because you want to keep the things you change, too. Writing in ink is also important when you have to use your steno pad as evidence in a hearing or review meeting.

Your To-Do Lists are where you record short term goals. These are probably the best organizing tools in your work kit. They should have four columns:

Start Date	Objective	Payoff	Done Date

Figure 3: To Do List

This journey will not be boring. There will be scary times and joyful times as you travel with me and become a consummate manager, a WORKPLACE CHAMPION!

John Smithman, Vancouver, Canada

Stage 1: Build a Solid Base For Your Growth

your first days on the job: a good time to plant seeds

TOPICS

First Communications Build Confidence
The Notebook
Looking Good and Fitting In
Assess the Workflow
Who's Your Predecessor?
Selling Skills
Serving Your Boss
Paradigms (habits of thought)
Groups and Teams
The Timeline Tool
Knowing Your People
{you} Inc.
Your Talented Workgroup

First Communications Build Confidence

This is a good time for the confident new supervisor to learn the lay of the land. Who will work with you and what will the organization support? Now is a good time to be a "curious detective" and ask the naive questions that you're expected to ask and some questions that no one will expect.

QB1. What will you do in your first few weeks after promotion?

You are the new supervisor. People are watching you. Some things they'll expect you to do. Some things no one will expect.

1. A critical first step. Interview your new boss to learn the expectations of your work, work schedule, expected reports, and meetings schedule.

2. Observe and listen to what goes on around you. Get a notebook (I use my steno pad) write the start date on the cover. Begin the habits that will carry you forward. Record work-related items.

3. Get a calendar to record your appointments. I use a desktop calendar because it's handy and others can check where I am when I'm out of my office.

7

4. Do not personalize your office. No photos, paintings or trinkets; just the tools of the job.

5. Interview your workers and work colleagues. I'll describe how, what and why later.

QB2. What are 4 things your boss expects during your early days?

Anticipate what your boss expects from you during your first few days. Here's some advice.

1. Do not make any changes yet. Observe, listen, and learn.

2. You're expected to introduce yourself to your work group and your co-workers. Interview your staff/workers, get to know them. Remember that first impressions can be misleading - they could be on good behavior; or nervous and on bad behavior. Describe their actions (without interpretation) in your notebook*.

3. You're expected to meet with your boss. Ask your boss questions, but not too many, one or two a day would be acceptable. Note the answers. Demonstrate your insight and intelligence by the questions you ask. Put yourself in your boss's shoes. Use your empathy to predict his or her position on matters.

4. You're expected to develop a strategy for doing your job. Do a full day's work; arrive and leave on time. Set the standard now. Do not come early or stay late.

The Notebook

The proper use of a notebook During my career, I was fortunate to have received some police training. I was impressed with their standards for using notebooks. Within reason, I applied these standards to my own handling of notebooks in my workplace. For example, here's Wikipedia on the use of a police officer's pocket note book (PNB), "All PNBs are subject to the same rules of disclosure as other confidential documents, and must contain everything deemed relevant to police work. Each new entry is marked with the day and date in capital letters, and is ended with a line covering the entire width of the page, along with the officer's signature. No information may be removed, and all corrections must be made by striking the incorrect entry with a line and inserting the correct entry with the officer's initials. Time must be written in 24-hour style, and any gaps left at the end of a line must be filled by a horizontal line to show that the gap was not created by the removal of a word. Many forces also require directly-quoted speech to be written in capitals."

"When an officer needs to record information in his notebook, the following are required by several forces:

- Time of day

- Exact or approximate location

- Offence or occurrence

- Names and addresses of offenders, victims or witnesses

- Action taken by the officer involved (e.g. arrests)."

"Some forces require the officer to write down what he or she said during the incident. Also, because it is not appropriate for an officer to interpret the meaning of a person's words or body language, the notes are limited to copying words and describing actions. For example, 'He replied, "No" in a very loud voice, while stamping his foot on the floor.' Not, 'He was mad when he answered, "No"'. It is better to allow the judge or jury to interpret the mood of the speaker from your neutral description of his actions."

"Although this description of the use of a notebook was developed for its use as evidence in a trial, keep the rules in mind as you use a notebook at your workplace. If there is a possibility of another person, such as a Human Resources or Union representative reading your notes of a meeting with an employee, then follow the standards listed above. Another good reason for following these standards merges with my belief that you should never say anything in private that you wouldn't say in public. This especially applies to the interpretation of feelings."

QB3. What are 5 things you expect from your new boss during the first few weeks?

Ask your boss to help you get established in your new workplace. He can support you by introducing you to your new staff and co-workers.

Your new boss should provide you with a clean and safe workspace, proper equipment and a phone list of suppliers and customers. When you think customers, include both internal and external ones. Internal customers are the ones that you serve inside your organization.

Ask your boss for an overview of the company and your unit's workflow from supplies and raw materials to customer satisfaction.

Your boss should give you guidance and explain the expectations of your unit and yourself generally: tasks and results expected.

Ask for a schedule for ongoing 1:1 review meetings. It's good practice to establish a schedule of meetings with your boss to report on your tasks and projects, to ask questions and to learn how to serve better. It's never convenient to drop in during work time to ask how to do something or to report on your activities. These types of meetings are considered bad time management.

A pre-scheduled half hour each week is a communication opportunity that will benefit you both. It saves you both time because it alleviates all those little interruptions that can take away your job focus. I have found that even though I might have wanted an answer a few days ago, waiting for my weekly meeting gives me time to think or research and find the answer for myself without bothering my boss. Then, when our meeting time arrives, I can say, "I found the answer on my own. So, unless you have something for me, we can delay our meeting until next week." You are both winners.

QB4. What do your workers expect from you and how should you respond?

They will appreciate a chance to meet you privately and learn a bit about your background [limit this to a brief list of your main qualifications for the job]. They may also want to tell you what kind of work they prefer, what skills they have that may not have been used in the past and may appreciate a change. Set up a regular 1:1 meeting time, as you did with your boss; for the same reasons.

Ask them about their equipment: its suitability for their work; and its maintenance condition. Tell them what you expect of them generally, it may be too early for specifics.

Be conscious that they will be watching and interpreting your body language. They have little else to judge at this stage. Communicate your sincerity, curiosity, respect and fairness.

QB5. How will you act toward your peers (other supervisors)?

This is similar to your meetings with your workers: introduce yourself (your experience, skills, ambitions); schedule times for future consultations; and state your intention to support them.

QB6. What policies will you implement on Day 1?

Set the standard for behaviors: show courtesy, respect, curiosity. Otherwise do not set any new policies.

Looking Good and Fitting In

It doesn't take much to look good and fit-in, because your promotion tells people that you must have something of value or it wouldn't have happened. But they don't know what you have yet. So, they will be paying close attention to how you look, what you do and what you say.

QB7. How will you dress for work?

Rule of thumb: Dress as well or slightly better than others at your level, but... don't guess. Ask your boss.

QB8. How will you behave toward your employees?

Always behave respectfully towards others. Be curious; you can learn a lot from them about the job, about their aspirations, about what motivates them. Their motivations will be keys to your future dealings with them.

QB9. How will you behave toward your colleagues?

Your colleagues will be important members of your company team, later on.

They are sounding boards for your company goals. You will include them in your plans for building consensus on changes. They could be your allies or defenders of the company line. Again, I recommend you take a stance of curiosity. Be interested in them and their goals. Look for clues and build links to their working styles.

QB10. How will you behave toward your boss?

Be curious about work goals, accomplishments, current activities. Show a genuine interest. Asking thoughtful questions will cement a good, ongoing relationship with your boss.

QB11. What's the most important thing to remember when talking about anyone's performance?

When speaking about a worker's performance, always talk as if that worker is listening.

If you are required to give feedback on a person's performance, praise publicly and criticize privately. People don't do anything for the wrong reasons. They do it for the right reasons, in their own minds. Uncover those reasons before filling in your own interpretations. This practice will serve you well in the days and weeks to come.

Assess the Workflow

The better you understand an organization's workflow, the easier it is for you to fit into that flow. Always accommodate the existing workflow first, before suggesting change. Be sure you fully understand the benefits of the current operation, before offering alternatives.

As new supervisor, you have a unique advantage. You can ask naive questions to help you learn the game, by playing Curious Detective. For example, "This may seem like a dumb question, but how long have we been doing things this way, and how successful is it?"

QB12. What is the best way to evaluate the standard work schedule?

Ask the boss, ask the workers, ask the colleagues and then draw your own conclusions based on your experience. Refer back to your current conclusions again after a few weeks. This will be your performance guide. Write down your best guesses about the answers to this question. Then confirm them by consulting with your boss privately at the first opportunity.

QB13. What are the established working systems?

Established systems deserve respect. They are the result of trial and error. Trial and Error are slow and painful, but they are effective. The systems are systems for good reason. Learn them and discover the history behind them. The fact that you are asking about the systems and their histories will build your own credibility in the eyes of others. And it will probably lead to some system re-thinking by the people you consult.

List the established systems. Do not consider changing them until after several months. Established systems are established for good reason. Be sure that you have good reasons, supported by your boss, before considering changes.

QB14. How are the established working systems effective?

Well this is the key question, isn't it? The assumption is that they are effective. Otherwise, make a note to address this with your boss when the time is right during your ongoing review meetings with him.

QB15. What does it mean if the employees are not consistently following the established systems?

I've seen elements of established systems altered by employees in large companies where they are not free, or don't know how, to share the challenges they see. With good intentions, employees may secretly substitute system elements.

If you discover this behavior, assume that workers have discovered weaknesses and have tried to repair them. Carefully inquire with an open mind and do your best to facilitate resolution of the systemic weaknesses.

Newly installed systems that look good on paper may be "kept in a drawer" by employees because they don't buy them. A new way of doing things must be sold to both the management and the workers. System-shifting by workers occurs in companies where communication between workers and top management is weak.

QB16. What can be done better?

Make notes in your notebook about the pros and cons of both systems. Prioritize the systems by their impacts on the bottom line. What do the substitutions address? Play curious detective. Ask obvious questions like, "How does each method affect profits or company resources?"

QB17. How is workflow tracked?

The sophistication of the tracking system varies amongst companies. The measures can be based on activity or on results. Are results measured by profit, volume, weight or something else?

Who's Your Predecessor?

Remember that someone has probably been here before you. You may learn a great deal from this person, directly or indirectly. Here are a few questions to consider as you step into your new position.

QB18. What can you learn from your predecessor?

You can learn much from your predecessor, what to do or what not to do, depending on his experience with the company.

An interview with your predecessor may be very helpful. If you have an opportunity to meet privately - off the job site - then take it. Be aware how it might appear to others. You may want to clear it with your boss first. Don't take notes. Mentally file away what you learn from such a meeting.

Even if you decide against the meeting, you can often learn a lot just by keeping your eyes and ears open as people talk about your predecessor. You can pick up the good and bad things he did. Whether his reputation is good or bad, the information you get could save you a lot of time. Carry on what was done well and avoid what was not done well.

QB19. What are the advantages and disadvantages of your predecessor's systems and metrics?

Ask. Take note of the answers, for these answers are justifications for your future choices. Advantages and disadvantages must be listed as to their impact on the workflow. Make note of how the impact was measured and what are your thoughts about how the systems can be adjusted to build the advantages and reduce the disadvantages.

QB20. What were the challenges and strengths within the last supervisor's methods?

Ask the question and note how the answers can guide your future decisions. Your analysis of his methods may offer alternatives to your own planning.

QB21. What did your predecessor do best?

What legacies were established? The answer may suggest a course for you to follow. We can always learn from the behaviors of those who walked the path before us.

QB22. Considering your predecessor's challenges and opportunities, what are logical goals to promote?

Goals are the children of Challenge and Opportunity.

Create goals by linking challenge and opportunity. Write them out in two parallel lists draw lines between those that seem to fit together. Prioritize your goals by their benefits to the company. Tackling each goal separately, consider how to gain the support of others in its achievement. Your success is based largely on how well you help others meet their needs by what you do.

Use a well-known sales strategy. List the benefits of each goal and build sales pitches to win others' support, especially those who can oppose or weaken your progress. If people believe they will gain as well from your goal's achievement, they will boost you along the way.

Selling Skills

Professional salespeople watch their potential customers closely for clues to what they like and then these salespeople link product benefits to customer needs to obtain the customer's approval before attempting a sale.

So, obtaining buy-in for your plans to know who are the decision-makers, to discover their needs and build a presentation to show each decision-maker how your proposal will address their needs. (You'll learn the phenomenal power of building consensus in Stage 4 of this book (QC85).

Finally, get written support from each decision-maker, if you can. If you do a good selling job, these decision-makers will become your own goal achievement and implementation team!

QB23. How has the game changed since you got the job with respect to staffing, equipment, and environment?

It's time to take a reading. People have had a chance to assess your potential. Look for changes that reflect their confidence in you.

Everyone who has just received a promotion is anxious to know how they're doing. What do people think? Are they sorry for choosing you or are they confirmed in their choice? It may not be proper to ask for their impressions of you, but you can certainly get a hint by observing the changes around you.

My own experience: whenever I promoted or hired someone, I'd watch and listen to how the new person is fitting in. If the positive signs are there, I'd quickly take actions to support that new person and enhance their chances for success.

I might introduce them to key decision-makers, add staff to their team, or provide more equipment to ease their workload. This may be the only positive feedback you can get at this stage of the process.

Serving Your Boss

The one person in the best position to help you grow is your boss. That seems obvious, but it must be in your boss's best interest to see you grow. What's in it for your boss to help you grow?

Remember to always sell the actions you want another to take. Learn what motivates your boss. Then show him how you can serve him.

Now understand that you are not alone, you have a group of workers that can help you serve your boss. You can serve by developing a formal action plan for yourself and your work group. So, while it may seem like I spend a lot time at this stage advising you to learn the capabilities of your workers, this is very important. As you learn the strengths of your workers, you are building trust with them. You are giving them a peek into their future value as members of your winning team.

Paradigms (habits of thought)

Remember salesmanship! To sell effectively, you must place yourself in the mind and heart of your boss. The better you see things as your boss sees them, the easier it will be for you to develop your own service role to help him meet his goals. This is your fundamental purpose: to serve your boss. Internalize this paradigm. Adopt the paradigm of service towards everyone you meet.

As you get closer to your boss, you may see weaknesses. Don't let this diminish your impression of him. This is opportunity. Look for ways to strengthen your most important team: you and your boss.

As a general rule, adopt the paradigm of service toward everyone you meet.

Groups and Teams

At this Stage of the book, I think of the supervised workers as a controlled work group under your control. Later, I'll refer to them as a team. A work group is uncoordinated workers who need individual direction for their achievements. A self-directed and self-motivated team takes on both role and intention for themselves independently.

This book contains sub-goals, such as the group-to-team transition process and the development of success strategies and universal tools such as the sales strategy just introduced into the goal achievement process as integrated practices that lead to workplace championship.

QB24. What are your boss's long term objectives for your work group?

How does your boss measure your value? Looking at yourself through his eyes, what does he see in you? in your work group?

Your value, generally, is in how you can help him achieve his goals. What skills or knowledge do you have that you can apply to that end? You know your own assets and the strengths of your people, but you can't know what will help your boss until you know his goals.

17

For instance, if one of his goals is to build a customer service team, then ask him to describe what he sees as the role of that team. How will he measure their success? Keep your meeting focused on one long term goal at a time until you have a full picture. Only then will you be able to assign tasks accordingly. Here's a great tool for getting the answers to the long term objective question.

The Timeline Tool

Here's what you do. Ask for a meeting to learn your boss's long term objectives. Sit down with him and draw a horizontal line on a page in your notepad. Write "0%" on the left end of the line and "100%" on the right end. Explain that the line represents the amount of work to be done between the beginning and the end of a project.

Let's use the customer service team as a sample project. Write that along the top of the line.

Ask your boss to mark the line at a point that he judges to be the current project progress position. He may believe that he's halfway there. So he marks the line at the 50% point. Draw a vertical line down from that point to the bottom of the page.

Now work together writing on the left side of the vertical line. List the things that have already been done to get to the 50% point. On the right side of the line, list the things still to be done to complete the project. Those last items are your tasks to-do list to reach the goal of having a customer service team.

Now, do this for each of his long term goals. You may need more than one meeting to get them all converted to objectives for you and your group.

QB25. How will you discover your workgroup's strengths?

Your job as superVISOR is to overSEE the activities of your workers. As you begin to know your boss's objectives, you will begin to assign work to those workers who are most able to do it. You know what you can do well, but how do you find out what your group members can do well.

The best way that I've found is to ask them to tell you stories. When the time is right, ask each worker to tell you about a time when they faced a work challenge. What was the challenge and how did they deal with it? Now listen for the "strengths and talents" and make notes on your notepad. When you have a good idea of their strengths, you can ask more focused questions that match what you know about their strengths.

QB26. What are your employees' opportunities working as a group?

Now that you know what the boss wants to achieve and you have your worker's strengths in mind, it's a simple matter of aligning strengths to tasks. You have learned enough from your discussions to be able to explain clearly to each worker what must be done and how it will be measured.

QB27. What are your employee's weaknesses working as a group?

After you have built the task list from your meetings with your boss, and have identified the matching strengths within your group, you will have a list of tasks that are left without matching strengths. That list is your work group's weaknesses.

IDEA: Here's an opportunity for you to work with your peers in other departments. If they have also developed a list of their workers strengths, they may be able to help you fill your needs for specific strengths by sharing their workers through temporary assignments.

QB28. What are your work group's challenges?

The challenge in most work groups is a lack of resources to use in their work. There are five categories of resources: time control, equipment, material, people and technique. The first and last can be taught. The middle three must be purchased or borrowed. Later, you will learn how to use what you've learned so far to get those resources.

QB29. How can you help your boss achieve his or her objectives through the work of your group?

Interviewing the boss is an opportunity missed by most new employees.

You now have the tools to help with your request for the resources. Help your boss prioritize his objectives. (You will learn how to prioritize a list of items using the PRIORITY TOOL described in the answer to QC84.) Next, negotiate to obtain the resources you will need to achieve his projects. This is work planning.

The result is a well-understood project plan that has the backing of your boss. It includes a clear description of the project's goal and the value of that goal to your boss. It includes how the achievement will be measured. It also includes a description of the resources that will be used and their costs, to compare to the beneficial value of the project. You have a very important role to ensure that the returns are greater than the costs.

QB30. What did you learn when you interviewed your boss?

Interviewing your boss is a great opportunity missed by most new employees. They are usually interviewed for the job and that's the last time they speak with their boss, until there's a problem.

Did you know that many workers are hired because they show the initiative to courteously interview the interviewer?

After the boss interview, read through your notes. Be sure you understand the meaning behind your boss's contributions. Did you learn what motivates your boss? What kinds of things please him? How does he like to receive project reports from you? When asked the right questions during a sales interview, a customer will tell you what he wants to hear from you to help you close the sale.

QB31. What are your boss's professional goals?

Professional goals are more personal than organizational goals. What are his ambitions? What would he like to have time for, to grow his own skills? Make a note to yourself about what you can do to help provide that time. Each worker has four areas of strength: knowledge, attitude, skills, and talents. How can you help your boss grow in these areas? These will add value to his personal assets and give him more options in his career.

QB32. What are the challenges and opportunities from your boss's perspective?

The better your empathy, the easier it will be to communicate and plan with your boss. Empathy is the ability to walk in the shoes of another; to see the world through their eyes; and to sense what they are sensing. The more interest you show in the world of another, the more interest they will show in your world. Empathy is one of the five most desired traits that managers want in their workers. [Refer to the 5 Most Desired Traits of the IDEAL Employee list in **Stage 4: Planning**.]

Listen to how your boss talks about the challenges and opportunities. The words used will tell you a lot about your boss's feelings towards these challenges or opportunities. There are many who believe the words chosen to describe challenges especially will reveal the attitude and the character of an individual.

Be sure to restate your boss's descriptions in positive terms. For example, when you hear the word "frustration", repeat the sentiment using a word like "fascination". Using a positive word helps us refocus on a "problem," shifting it to a "challenge" instead. This refocusing guides our thoughts towards solutions, because the word "challenge" itself implies that there is a solution. Problems are barriers. Challenges are opportunities. Make notes in your notebook of the words that your boss uses and write down alternative words that you will use to encourage positive (solution-based) thinking.

Knowing Your People

Your workers are your partners in performing the work of the organization. They rely as much on you as you do on them. You are their supervisor which literally means that you over-see them. There's a responsibility in that. What do they need from you in return for what you need from them? The next few questions will help you learn the answer.

QB33. What questions will you ask each individual?

This is a good time to use the {you} INC. process, which begins with establishing a respectful base for the questions that follow. This fact-finding exercise builds trust. Find a quiet, private area for the following discussion. Start like this.

{you} Inc.

Write their full name on your notepad, add 'INC.' and underline it. Say, "Let's assume that you are a corporation, with unique assets, that are worth a certain value. Currently you're renting out these assets to the company. In the future, if you were to decide to work for another, you would take your assets with you, wouldn't you?" . . . Wait for a response, before proceeding.

"I'm going to ask you questions about your assets in six areas. Is that okay?

The first area is Know-How."

KNOW-HOW "This is your knowledge, your education and training, your talents, and your experience. Tell me about your Know-How." ... Comment positively as you listen. Make brief notes about their qualifications and learning experiences. Then ask, "If you could have more know-how in any area what would that be?"

ENERGY "This is your level of endurance. Some work seems to fit us to a tee; we feel energized while doing it. While other types of work take away our power." Listen and record. "What type of work energizes you?"

TIME "This refers to our use of Time. Do you find there's enough time in the day to get everything done? When do you prefer to work? Some people do their best work in the morning; others prefer to work in the evenings. Is there a time of day when you are most productive? If you could have more time, how much time would you ask for each day?"

CONCENTRATION "This is about your working environment. What interrupts your work? How do you deal with interruptions? Is there some work that you do where nothing interrupts you because you enjoy it so much?"

IMAGINATION "This is about your ability to foresee the future, to see the path that will transform today into tomorrow. It involves the setting of goals and building of plans to achieve those goals. How is your Imagination?"

DECISIONS "What is your process for making decisions? Spontaneous, calculating, or with the help of others? Please tell me how you like to make decisions."

"Assuming we could improve about 10% in one area, what area is best for you? What would a 10% increase in that area do for you?"

While conducting this interview, make clear notes on your pad or notebook. Keep your notes positive and complimentary. Be sure to let the individual see the validating notes you are taking.

After conducting this special interview, I usually continue and launch into preparing a Formal Goals and Objectives agreement. This gives us both something to work on together.

QB34. How will you log and record the results of each interview?

This is the review of your interview. You will log the time and results of your interview in your notebook and later, transfer the information into a working file for each worker.

QB35. What are the important facts to have in each worker's personal file?

Here are some facts to preserve in a private place for your use only:

• Contact data: home, cell phone, email address, home address.

• Important people in their lives: spouse, children, idols, heroes.

• What influences and motivates them: people, money, family, security? They'll tell you if you ask them.

QB36. How will you record each worker's skills and talents?

This is very important because it will help you to choose the best assignments for them to carry out. Skills come from training; talents come from experience. How can you help them use their skills?

QB37. How will you record and track each worker's progress?

I assign a notebook to each employee where I keep notes of their assignments and progress that I see and hear. These notes will save you time later when you want to review their work before recognizing and rewarding them for their good work. Remember to keep notes on the positives in their performance. This will serve you well if you have to discipline them too, as you will see in Stage 2 when you may need to have a disciplinary meeting to correct the wrongs that they will very likely do, especially if they take risks. Taking risks is how people grow.

QB38. Do you know the names of each worker's significant family members?

Make it your goal to know and remember the significant people in your employee's life. You honor your employees by doing this. Show interest in them and they will show interest in you.

QB39. What are their personal motivations and hopes for their job?

What motivates your employee? Not in a general way, but in a specific way. Is it money, self-respect, work pride, a desire to grow their personal assets, a personal promotion in future, recognition and rewards, pleasure that will repay them for their time and effort at work?

QB40. Is each worker doing the work they like and qualify for?

Are your employees properly matched to their work? If not, consider how to make it so. Highly productive employees are doing the work they are qualified to do in the environment they prefer. You can ask the "experience" questions I introduce in the You-Inc section on interviewing your employees to determine the skills and preferred working environments of each employee.

Your Talented Work Group

I've discovered that each employee has unique talents. As their manager, your job is to discover these talents and learn how to apply them to the job. You are like TV's MacGyver who had to work with the materials available to him as he devised a plan for success. He would create miracles with these materials as he built plans that made the best use of each part in the construction of the whole.

There are unlimited ways to achieve the results you desire. Never feel that you don't have the best tools and resources. Your mind is capable of finding ways to work well with what is available. It is MIND OVER MATTER: if you don't mind, it won't matter. Think of the word 'mind' as a verb, not a noun. Think "My Mind is a Verb" and put this new paradigm to work. There's an old saying, "A good workman knows his tools." Know your workers' talents and how to apply them!

QB41. What's your schedule for meeting with the workers, both as a group and individually?

People grow or shrink over time, depending on feedback. We learn best when we are challenged and motivated to take risks in a safe environment. The best learning is continuous learning where we get a regular diet of opportunities to stretch our own talents through regular exposure to new ideas followed by thoughtful reflection and feedback.

Create an environment for progressive applied learning by scheduling regular, scheduled meetings with groups and with individuals for reporting, review, reflection and recognition of the success or failure of talent stretching activities. With repetition, these meetings will be welcomed, not feared like many review meetings are in a workplace where they happen rarely. As you conduct these meetings, you model and teach your employees powerful leadership principles.

While I highly recommend a positive approach to supervision and management, we can't ignore examples of shortcomings.

QB42. Are there gaps in the skills or talents of your workers?

Assess your employees for opportunities in their weaknesses. Locate areas for improvement in each individual as well as in the whole group. Use the regular 1:1s to address these growth opportunities by sharing the benefits of building new talents.

QB43. Are they group-like or team-like as a force? What makes you think that?

Learn the differences between groups and teams. What motivates groups, teams? How do groups plan and work? How do teams plan and work? Where are opportunities in groups? In teams?

There's a story about a horse pull contest that illustrates the value of teams over individuals. A contest was staged where two horses performed individually and pulled a total weight of 4500 pounds each on a sled when they did it individually. Someone decided to see how much they would pull as a team and hitched them together. They pulled 12,000 pounds!

As you read this story, consider what would happen if they were hitched together facing in opposite directions. Their efforts would cancel each other's out. What would have to be in place for a team of employees to behave better together than they would as individuals?

A group is a number of individuals working on their own, with little or no collaboration. If a group is called a team, it implies that they have some skills that compliment or augment each other.

What other things would you want to see, for a team to work better than a group? Compatible personalities, good communication, complementary skills, similar interests or experiences -- the list is long. Think about it.

Put a group of individuals together, observe their interactions and measure their results. Mix them up and try again as you build effectiveness into your workplace.

QB44. What are the untapped resources of your workers?

As a supervisor, you should look for untapped skills in your employees. Monitor not just the work they are assigned to do, but look at opportunities for variety in their assigned tasks that may reveal some untapped resources.

My own experience, as an example: Phil, one of my employees had told me that he came to Canada from Southeast Asia to become a TV journalist. He went specifically to Toronto's Ryerson University to learn this skill. After graduation, he couldn't find work in his chosen field and instead he accepted a telephone receptionist job at our company in Vancouver.

He was communicating alright, but he still had unfulfilled desires. So, I gave him some writing assignments. He loved this work and performed very well.

Later, as opportunities for more writing assignments appeared, guess who happily accepted the assignments? Eventually, when my executive secretary retired, I asked Phil to take her job. He jumped at the opportunity.

QB45. How would your group's results improve if you used their untapped resources?

If Phil was assigned to work in a group project, what role would he do the best? Probably a role that required recording and reporting skills.

Having one person in the group responsible for reporting begins to transform the group into a team. A primary team responsibility is to report their progress to the outside world. And not everyone is a good reporter. Assigning that responsibility to Phil would help to ensure the team's success.

QB46. How would your group perform if they were a team?

If they had the right leader, your group could perform better as a team.

A team is a group of people who work together to achieve a goal. Members are selected for their talents that can be blended in the pursuit of that goal.

There are four things required for a team to work well. They must have a well-defined goal. They must be able to blend their skills and talents. They must be able to lead themselves. They must have the resources to accomplish their tasks.

Summary (Stage 1)

So far, we have begun to define Developmental Supervision. You've been introduced to Creative Thinking Frames (Insights) and basic tools you'll need as a supervisor, to learning the expectations of those around you through communication, and how to fit into your new workplace. You've begun to assess systems effectiveness and how to serve by learning your boss's goals and expectations of the work group you supervise. Then, you began to determine how your group can benefit both your boss and the organization.

Next you'll look at the work environment and its readiness for change.

Stage 2: Understand the Workplace

look outside your immediate work group

TOPICS

How to Identify a Saboteur
Ed's Story
Your Company's Working Style
Consider Roles and Responsibilities
Weekly Review Meetings. Remove the Rumors

Before going outside, I check the weather. If it's raining, I wear a raincoat or carry an umbrella. If it's sunny, I wear sun protection or carry an umbrella for shade. If it's cold, I dress warmly. If it's warm, I don't dress warmly. You get the picture. It helps to know what the climate is before you enter the environment.

Each company has its own personality. Some companies are outgoing, others are reserved. Some are task oriented and some are people-oriented. The style of the company sets the stage for your style. Conform and you will fit in. Don't conform and you will cause ripples. What is the climate of your organization?

Are there storms brewing or is the weather just fine? First, we'll look at your co-workers and then we'll consider the company.

How to Identify a Saboteur

It's nice to be surrounded by supporters, but someone who wanted your new job may be upset that they missed out and may react strangely.

Saboteurs can appear without warning and they may not think of themselves as saboteurs. They're just normal people acting to meet their personal needs. There's no such thing as a person doing something for the wrong reason. People do what they do for the right reasons - in their own mind. [Later we will examine human needs and empathy in Stage 3: Put Your Plans in Motion.]

However, it's important that you identify potential saboteurs early when you have a chance to understand and deal with the challenges before you get hurt unexpectedly. It's often just a matter of understanding their motives and helping them meet their needs in a different way.

Ed's Story

Early in my career, I was promoted to supervisor over a more senior worker. I didn't have to look for the saboteur in that case! He revealed himself clearly, "John, you got *my* job. I've worked hard to get that job and now I'm going to do everything I can to see you fail!"

Ed was obviously hurt; and I had to figure out how to handle his unexpected challenge. At 37, I was 25 years younger than he and I was a part time computer science student.

My boss promoted me to supervisor because he wanted me to 'computerize' the office. We were handling hundreds of wooden boxes filled with paper records that were sorted by hand and stapled together. It was very hard to keep track of them and records were getting lost regularly. My boss asked me to set up a computer database to control about 200,000 office records.

Ed, with his experience, was a great asset to the office and I didn't want to lose him. So I thought about how to deal him in.

At the time, I was reading a copy of Donald and Eleanor Laird's book, SIZING UP PEOPLE. In particular, this text caught my eye: "The average person or 'common man' is a myth, created by statistics and kept alive by politics. We are all eccentric to an extent. Part of the supervisor's job is to note these variations and to stimulate each worker to make the best use of his own abilities."

Ed's strengths were in his knowledge and experience. He was the go-to guy whenever we had a problem to solve. As a vocal critic, he was forever pointing out other's mistakes. His quick mind and troubleshooting skills were amazing. He could be a big help in setting up the new database system. But he had given public notice that he wasn't going to learn computers this late in his career. And besides, he 'hated' computers.

29

So, here's what I did. The other staff members were assigned to enter all the records into their computer terminals for nearly a year; and while building the database, they made plenty of data-entry errors. Each week, we received sorted print-outs of the week's entries from the computer office. I told Ed that the 'dumb' computer had no ability to correct entry errors. We had to do that ourselves.

In a few weeks, Ed began looking over my shoulder as I checked the lists for errors. He was a perfectionist and it wasn't long before his troubleshooting skills kicked in. But, to fix the errors, he had to learn how to use the computer terminals. Soon, he lost touch with his anger against me and became the Keeper of the Database." ... I arranged for him to get a pay raise to reward him for his new role.

. . .

A few years later at his retirement party in his farewell speech, he said, "When John was promoted to office supervisor I put him on notice and vowed to see him fail. I'm glad now that he didn't fail, because John was the best thing to happen to this office."

I tell this story because it's a happy ending to a common challenge in the workplace: misdirected anger due to personal pain. With the help of Dr. Laird's book, I was able to size-up Ed's skills and attitude and find a way to help him win the praise and recognition he deserved.

Use empathy to resolve people problems that don't make sense.

QW47. How do your new employees feel about your new role?

Supportive? Alienated? How can you find out?

At appropriate times, like when you are together out of the eavesdrop of others, ask a question like the following: "I've seen your qualifications. What would you do if you were in my shoes right now?" Wait for the reply. Give them plenty of time to answer.

Pause before speaking again. Carefully consider their answer. Then follow up with probing questions like: How? What would be the benefits of that? When's a good time to do it? How can you play a role in this? What would be the challenges, if any?

If their answer suggests they may stand in your way, now is the best time to understand their motives and begin amelioration. Make notes in your notebook for review later in a quiet moment. Think positively about it. There's time to work on it, proactively.

QW48. How can you help them achieve their own objectives?

Know each employee's personal objectives. Understand what motivates them: the logic and the emotion, the thoughts and the feelings. Not only what they will think about their achievements, but also how they will feel. That is your leverage for getting things done for them as well as for yourself.

QW49. What can they teach you over the next few weeks and months that will help your progress?

About THEIR work...

In Stage 1, you interviewed your workers about their know-how, skills, talents, training and experience. You discovered that they were quite talented in areas that you hadn't expected to find. You found their "championship".

As you begin to act on this knowledge and assign them to work on what they know and understand, you will see an increase in their productivity and a relaxation in their posture.

You may also learn the best way to do the job because you are watching and learning from a champion. They become your benchmarks for the job.

Look for chances to publicly praise good performance when you see it. To maintain your objectivity, always give good (in public) or bad (in private) feedback that recognizes the behavior, and not the person.

Just like technicians learn how to use their tools effectively, you are learning the effectiveness of your people.

About YOUR work...

They will help you grow as a natural leader. You have the privileged opportunity to test unique ways of motivating and training people in the workplace. You'll learn what works and how it may work differently for each individual.

Your employees are great sources of company history and new ideas. They are closer to the work than you are and know more about the challenges and opportunities in that work than you do.

Ask good questions and pay proper attention to the answers. Probe and try to read between the lines. If there are problems creeping up in the workplace, your employees will tell you -- often in subtle ways. Listen carefully.

QW50. How will you communicate with employees? What style or environment is best?

This is another area where you can experiment. I have found that certain environments or times of day support good dialogue. For example, with some employees, going for a walk in the park or along the shore encouraged good communication. An office -- yours or his -- may work better. Group meetings promote good communication, as in brainstorming where each person's views can activate others'. Brainstorming is group thinking.

Personal Behavior Style filters communication as well as collaboration. Find a quick way to assess style on the next page.

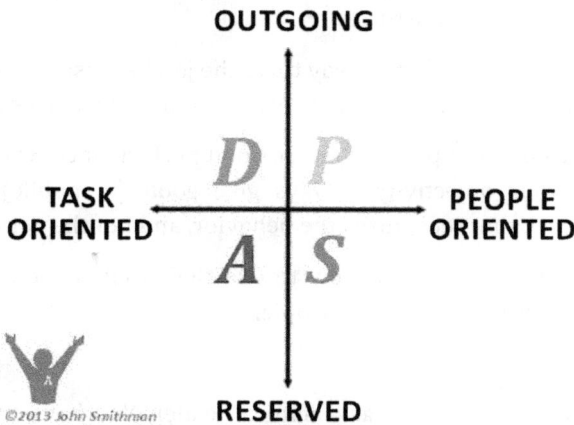

Figure 4: Work style

Create a table with four quadrants like this. Label the two crossing scales as **Behavior** (reserved/outgoing) and **Environment** (task-oriented/people-oriented).

Place your subject's name on the table where he seems to fit the best. For each employee, answer four questions about their observed behavior and preferred working conditions. Is the BEHAVIOR reserved or outgoing? Rate on a scale of from 1 to 10: with 1 as quite reserved and 10 as very outgoing?

WORKING CONDITIONS: Does the employee like working on tasks or working with people? On a scale from 1 to 10, how task or people-oriented are they? 1 is fully task-oriented and 10 is very people-oriented.

The four quadrants have labels to describe their preferred performance roles: Quadrant 1 (Outgoing, Task-oriented) is D for **Decider**; Quadrant 2 (Outgoing, People-oriented) is P for **Promoter**; Quadrant 3 (Reserved, People-oriented) is S for **Supporter**; and Quadrant 4 (Reserved, Task-oriented) is A for **Analyzer.**

Labeling people like this may seem trivial, but as a quick guide it provides you an advantage when communicating or working with someone. Later, I'll show you how to put teams together for specific tasks using DPSA style analysis.

These style labels suggest effective modes of communication. Deciders and Promoters tend to speak quickly, while Promoters and Supporters have a slower pace. Deciders and Analyzers tend to hide their feelings. Promoters are friendly. Supporters are warm. Analyzers like to be accurate and sound competent. You will learn to adjust your style to match the person you are communicating with.

Your Company's Working Style

Just like individuals, companies have styles too. Is your company out-going or reserved, task oriented or people oriented?

Using the DPSA Style Analysis process, take a moment to think about your company's style. Compatibility is the key to success when it comes to matching your style with your company's. Outgoing companies prefer to hire outgoing people.

Another way that your "style" can make things easier for you is in doing tasks or functions that favor your behavior style. Below, I have colored company departments according to the behavior style that seems to fit best for the work involved.

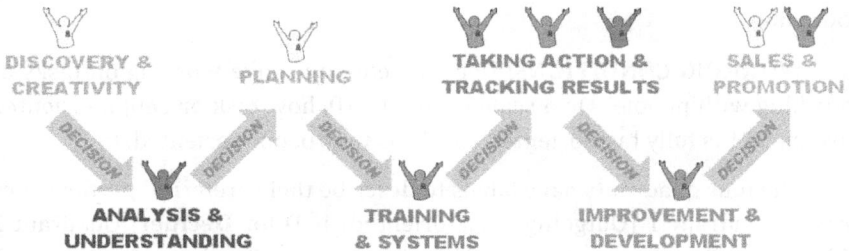

DISCOVERY &
CREATIVITY

PLANNING

TAKING ACTION &
TRACKING RESULTS

SALES &
PROMOTION

ANALYSIS &
UNDERSTANDING

TRAINING
& SYSTEMS

IMPROVEMENT &
DEVELOPMENT

Figure 5: Automate Success With Systems and Style

QW51. What are five ways that you could help your company increase their revenues?

There are three elements that influence consumer choice: Price, Quality and Service. More customers will buy if you lower the price, if you raise the quality or if you improve the service. Typically, companies can offer only two out of three without going broke.

So, to increase revenues look for ways to improve customer perceptions of price, quality and service. These elements are what customers perceive they are. So, if you can't lower the price, at least build a case to show that, compared to the value received, the price is low.

This story illustrates how an auctioneer added value to a violin he was trying to sell at a fair price.

He interrupted the auction for a moment to allow the violin's owner to play the instrument. After the audience heard the smooth sound quality and heart-felt notes coming from the violin, their bids rose sharply.

QW52. What are three ways that you can help your company save costs?

Increase effectiveness and efficiency and decrease the use of resources.

We increase effectiveness by improving our use of systems, equipment and people to reduce the cost of the five resources of TIME, ENERGY, MONEY, PEOPLE and TECHNOLOGY.

However, increasing efficiency doesn't necessarily save costs. We may be doing unnecessary things very efficiently. Efficiency should be increased only after we have raised the effectiveness of what we are doing. There's no sense in doing the wrong things very well.

Costs are odd things to measure without having something to weigh them against. If you spend a lot of resources to obtain more valuable resources, you are net-saving by spending.

QW53. How can your company promote its services better?

Communicate with your customers both generally and specifically: what we do for our customers' world and what we do for our customers. We are both blessed and cursed by so many media options these days. Many books are written on how to use the media to promote our products and services.

First determine your fair share of the customer base and then experiment. Take note of the style characteristics of your public and consider what product, services and means of communication would have the strongest impact on them.

Then try, test and take note of the results. I recently heard a marketer suggesting testing Tweets by time of day and day of week to measure the best response results.

I have tested brochures by writing them to appeal to each of the four behavior styles. When you give a presentation, always consider the four different style groups in your audience and include something for everyone.

QW54. How will you brainstorm with colleagues to find new ways to market your products?

Get several people together for the purpose of brainstorming a solution to a problem.

Brainstorming can have great results if you follow the basic rules of brainstorming. Ask people for ideas, no matter how ridiculous, within a time constraint. Record the ideas.

Ask people to think of ways to synthesize these ideas, no matter how ridiculous, "We could parade three small dogs down Main Street pulling a wagon with a poster of our newest product on it. Take photos and post them on social media, Facebook and Pinterest or send Tweets, to share the event with others."

Withhold any criticism until new ideas are exhausted or time has run out. You will be pleased with the results.

And, if nothing else, the brainstorm meeting will attract attention. At one of my clients' companies, after the news of a marketing brainstorming session got out, ideas came in from unexpected areas of the company's employee base.

Pay Attention To What You Want More Of.

QW55. How will you deliver the same results with fewer staff?

Simplify the work. Create systems. Design, modify or purchase new equipment to ease the workload. Ask the workers themselves for input.

Complicate the worker. Train new skills and change behavior or environment. We spoke of matching employees to tasks and environments for better productivity.

QW56. If you have a chance to sit down with the company CEO, what questions will you ask?

The Chief Executive Officer (CEO) can be the leader of a large organization, the owner of a small or medium-sized company or the president of an organization. I'll use 'CEO' in this answer to refer to any of these people.

CEOs drive the company. They are less concerned with detail than they are with company purpose and mission. On the following chart, see what's important to each manager in a typical company. Note that CEO's are mostly concerned with big picture: mission, purpose, public perceptions and serving shareholders. They receive regular summaries on operations, but their view is mostly outward.

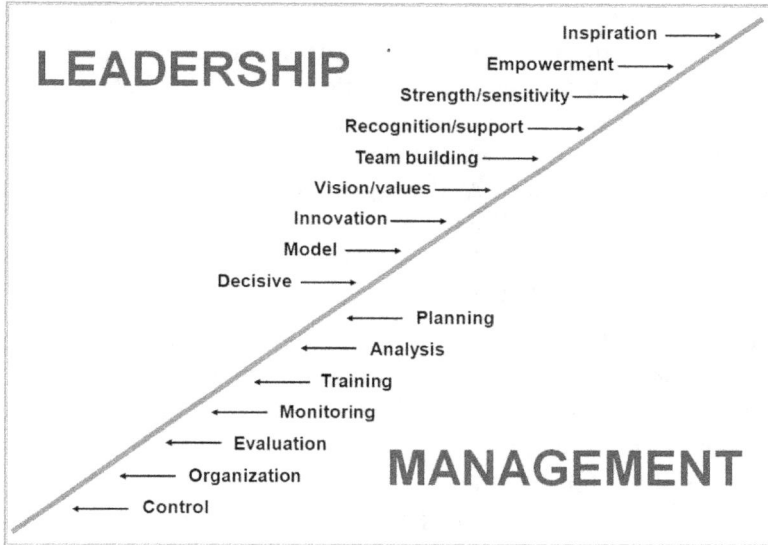

Figure 6: Management-Leadership Concerns

Structure your questions in a way that lets you assess how your role can support the CEO's goal.

What is the mission of this company? How would the public describe us? What are three key goals for the company? How do we work with other companies in three areas: enhancing the lives of our clients; protecting the environment; and rewarding our shareholders?

Consider Roles and Responsibilities

This is a good time to begin collaborating with your boss; to ensure that you are both on the same page. That you are doing what he/she wants you to do and that she approves of your progress. Arrange a series of scheduled 1:1 meetings to validate and ratify your activities while you learn the job. This is also a good time to learn the RACI lay of the land for your company. [Refer to Question 61.]

QW57. List your roles and responsibilities and get your boss's agreement on your list.

Ensure that none of your tasks are on your boss's list too, unless it requires both your efforts. A useful exercise to clear the air and promote understanding is to take two sheets of paper and label them as follows. Draw two lines on the page: one line vertically down the center of the page and one line horizontally across the center of the page, creating four quadrants. At the top left, write "My Roles"; and half way down on the left, write "My Responsibilities". At the top right, write "Your Roles". Halfway down on the right, write "Your Responsibilities". Now, each of you take some time privately to complete the forms you created, by noting each of your Roles and Responsibilities on the forms.

When you've finished, get together and compare notes. This is a good way to compare your perceptions of what should be done by whom. You can analyze the results. Are there roles or responsibilities that are carried out by both persons, when one person would do? Are there any important roles or responsibilities that are not carried out by anyone? Try using this simple exercise to clear the air between you and to remind each other of our cooperative relationships.

By the way, this exercise works so well that it is used by marriage counselors to clear the air between quarreling couples.

QW58. Have you prioritized your current job responsibilities by assessing their value in helping you to achieve your goals?

One of the most important time management tools is a priority list. The theory is that if you have only so much time to do things, it's best if you do them in order of which task is the most important to do next.

The key word here is "important." Important to whom? How do you define importance? For small tasks, the answer may be obvious. But for larger tasks? Maybe not so obvious. Take time to develop a list of criteria for this exercise.

Work may be judged by its effect on the company's profits, on the company's reputation, on the workflow, on your career. There are many criteria that can be used to measure the effect of any one task.

As it turns out, developing a priority list for a set of tasks or responsibilities is not a trivial task.

QW59. Which of your job roles could be performed better by someone else in your workgroup?

Always be aware that your career growth depends on your finding more valuable work to do and then doing it. This suggests that what you are doing now should be done by someone else or should not be done at all. Think carefully about this critical step in your development. The best time to discontinue a redundant job is at handover. That's when a discontinued job is not likely to be missed. If the job is important, then recognize its importance by reassigning it to someone new. By doing so, you are also recognizing the employee's importance.

QW60. Which jobs have no reason to be on your job list? How will you eliminate them?

Growing companies look for cost savings. A big ongoing expense is salaries. It's the first place owners look to reduce their expenses. They are always evaluating the cost of selling their goods and services.

Be prepared. As a supervisor you are in a good position to anticipate this. So look for it. Be a step ahead. Be prepared to justify salary expense with numbers to reflect the values, benefits and costs of all jobs including your own.

A good way to save costs is to ensure that jobs are being done well by the lowest paid positions. If you see a job on your list that could be done cheaper by someone who reports to you or by a part time worker, then check into it. Jobs that can be done better by someone below your pay rank should be done by them. The added benefit is experience for the employee who is moving up in the company.

QW61. How would you apply the RACI Method to assess job flow within your own work group?

The RACI Model RACI is an acronym for Responsible, Accountable, Consulted and Informed. The theory is that everyone working in an organization is playing at least one of those four roles. If not, they are not playing any role and maybe should not be an employee.

The exercise is straightforward. Create a table on a spreadsheet listing every important activity, task or decision of the working group in the left-most column. List the names of the employees in the top row, so that you have a box or cell at the intersection of each task list item and employee name. In that cell, write an R, A, C, or I.

When you're done, tally the list to assess the distribution of roles and responsibilities. There are certain key measures to consider:

Too many Rs: Person may be doing too much. Can the work be distributed?

No Rs or As: Should this function be eliminated? Is no one taking the initiative?

Too many As: Is this a decision bottleneck? Can accountability be shared?

Check qualifications: Is the person in each role qualified?

Too many Cs: Do so many people need to be consulted?

Too many Is: Who really needs to be informed?

Every cell has a letter: There shouldn't be. Too many Cs and Is perhaps? Reduce Cs to Is?

No spaces in column: Fingers in too many pots.

QW62. How will you approach your boss with the results of your RACI review?

RACI resolves unclear roles and multiple decision points if you act on the results. Some suggestions: Eliminate checkers checking checkers; rebuild the chart to encourage teamwork; place As and Rs at the lowest levels; Ensure that authority accompanies accountability; and minimize Cs and Is.

Review your results with your boss to help with planning or troubleshooting. This will also help to confirm the accuracy of your analysis. Other possible benefits of the RACI analysis is the redistribution of roles and responsibilities: re-organizing workers' geography throughout the workplace; reducing, reassigning or adjusting the workforce; and replacing or renewing equipment to save time, money and effort.

Weekly Review Meetings Remove Rumors

I refer to regular review meetings between an employee and supervisor as one-to-ones (1:1). This is a scheduled weekly one-hour meeting that provides a communication opportunity. It's a time to discuss successes, challenges and opportunities in the life of the worker. It's not a time to give orders or apply discipline to the worker. The meeting is for and about the worker. It builds valuable two-way trust. It's also an opportunity to examine and dispel or confirm company rumors.

QW63. What will you discuss at your weekly, one-hour 1:1 meetings?

It will be a coaching session. You are the coach; your employee is your champion. Your role is to discover and build your champion's skills. Motivate him to use those skills to benefit the company. With this mission in mind, here's a typical 1:1 meeting.

Begin with your observations of what was done well this week and its value to the company. Follow with some questions encouraging your champion to report on his own observation of his performance during the past week. Refer to his goals and to-do lists. He will likely be more critical than you. For example, "Are you pleased with your progress? Are there some things that you'd like to improve? I have some ideas to help you with that."

If you both feel there is room for improvement and that the time is right, offer your champion a gentle challenge to take it up a notch. Propose a way to measure the impact of his actions, preferably by measuring the change in results. Remember that it is also your duty to protect your champion and not force him to a point where he could be injured.

Many supervisors believe they should be forcing their workers beyond their limitations. They reason that even if they don't get everything done, they are least moving forward. This is a bad practice. It is not motivational for most people. It's like over-fueling a spaceship to the moon. The result? Overburdened vehicle being held back by the extra weight.

Sports analogies seem suitable when speaking about skills and performance. The language is similar, but the measures are different. A

Workplace Champion must stay aware of company values, goals and practices.

QW64. What is your plan for weekly work group meetings?

As supervisors, we begin with one worker or a small group of workers. Actions are independent for the most part. Projects are small, short-lived and limited. Group meetings will also be limited. Use group meetings to teach your workers how to have effective meetings. Be vigilant for distractions that can occur.

People have been having effective group meetings for hundreds of years. Plenty of books have been written about running good meetings. I've found answers in Robert's Rules of Order. This book is designed to provide a way to conduct business and get decisions made smoothly and quickly.

Without Robert's Rules, meetings can get out of hand. In-fighting and arguments can arise. Meetings can take much too long. The main purpose of a meeting is to share information and offer opportunities for the input of others. But I don't think I have ever been at a meeting where someone hasn't said after the meeting that they wish they would have had a chance to say something.

A meeting needs three elements to work well: a meeting Chair, a meeting Recorder, and a meeting Monitor. The Chair sets the agenda, starts and ends the meeting. A good approach is to state the meeting's purpose at the start and allow agenda changes only if agreed to by all parties. Keep meetings short and productive. Robert's Rules requires ideas to be wrapped in Motions. A Motion is a written statement of an action proposal that is read by the Chair for input from the participants as views for and against the Motion until it is time for a vote. Once voted upon, a Motion becomes an Order and the meeting Chair assigns someone to execute the Order.

QW65. Who, within your group, can be assigned to chair your meetings?

Encourage your co-workers to take turns running meetings. This is a great way to grow successors in your company. It also offers your co-workers a chance to experience what you feel as a supervisor.

As meeting chair they have to understand the purpose and impact of each decision; they must get things done through others; and they have to learn how to understand and influence decisions. It's great experience that will serve them for the rest of their career.

QW66. Describe your weekly 1:1 meeting with your boss.

This meeting is a chance to review and confirm your activities with your boss. It can be a weekly, monthly, or semi-annual meeting, as long as it is regularly scheduled.

Start by announcing to your boss that this is his meeting. He can write the agenda. You're here for him because you want to be sure that what you do in your job benefits him. You have allowed 30 minutes for the meeting, but if it takes longer, that's okay. You have planned some things to talk about; but again, it's his meeting.

So, how do you hope your 1:1 meeting goes? You hope to have an opportunity to brag about what you have accomplished in your job. You hope to share your current task list and confirm that its priority is correct. Your list should have an estimate of the time and other resources needed to complete each task. You should also have an estimate of the benefits to your boss and to the company of doing each task. There may be an opportunity to share some news about your workers or yourself. This will give your boss a chance to share some news with you, too.

Summary (Stage 2)

We studied the quality of our workers and our working environment, including the company's working style.

We looked at how to reduce costs and increase revenues. We learned the roles and responsibilities of key people; established weekly meetings to remove uncertainty and keep the peace; and we examined some systems that we will use to create our results.

Next, we move on to Stage 3: PUT YOUR PLANS IN MOTION.

Stage 3: Put Your Plans In Motion
time for organizational planning and development

TOPICS
Leadership Lesson from My Mom
Taking Stock
The Ideal Employee
How to Determine the IDEAL Employee
Assessing the Operation and Its People
Employee Turnover
Progressive Applied Learning (PAL)
IN-WIN-POUT-OUT
Basic Human Needs
Train-Drain - The Horizon Effect
Fine Tuning Performance
John's Story
Discipline - The Hard Decisions

Leadership Lesson from My Mom

When I was a teenager, I learned a critical lesson at my mom's Saturday night card parties. I'd learned to play Bridge so that I could fill in if someone didn't show up. Sixteen bridge players would occupy four card tables and change partners as they played throughout the evening, allowing each person to play four rounds of cards with each other player. Bridge Tallies provided both the plan and the score sheets.

At the end of the evening, Dad would calculate the scores to discover the first prize winner. So far, this is similar to the way most people held Bridge parties in those days. But, in our case, Mom made a difference!

On Friday afternoon, she'd take the bus 20 miles into town and shop at the five-and-dime store. She'd buy a number of small gifts: a comb, key chain, a mirror, other trinkets, ribbons and wrapping paper. When she arrived home she would wrap up each trinket and tie it with a ribbon.

On Saturday, after the game, Mom would serve beverages and cookies and Dad would tally the scores. While the guests enjoyed treats, Dad would announce the winners and hand out gifts. A gift for the player with the highest score, one for second place and for third place, a booby prize for the 'unselfish' person with the lowest score, a prize for the best dresser, one for the player with the funniest joke or story told during the evening, a prize for the nicest smile and so on. Mom had labeled a gift for each of her guests. She knew the value of recognition.

I didn't realize it at the time, but Mom taught me an important leadership lesson: pay attention to what you want more of; recognize the good in people. It was a rare day when they needed me to fill in for a missing player. Who could refuse an invitation to Mom's Bridge parties?

I've had a successful career based on Mom's example. Don't you hate it that most contests reward only the winners? One winner, and a whole bunch of losers. No wonder companies are in trouble. What about the player with the nicest smile? ...

Looking for the good in people is motivational for them *and* for you.

Taking Stock

You have built yourself a solid foundation and you have a good understanding of the company climate. You know the strengths and hopes of your employees, colleagues and boss. You have established a communication network within your company. You even have an idea of the potential of the company and a sense of your role in its future. Generally, your employees pass the TASTE test. That is, they have the credentials of ideal employees. They are TIME-savvy, have a positive ATTITUDE, are SKILLED in their jobs, practice TEAMWORK and demonstrate EMPATHY.

It's time now to set out your plans and activate them.

You will impact your organization by building on the strengths already present, creating consensus to support your plans, avoiding the scourge of large companies - *Employee Turnover*, building loyalty within your employee base, and showing them what you are capable of doing. You have good work habits that can be shared with others in the organization. You know that change is difficult for people to accept, so you will go slowly and use your best influencing style and selling skills.

First, you will analyze {the TASTE test, Employee Turnover Matrix} the people and then assess the organization's production {bottlenecks} and customer service {Meeting the Needs, Pleasing the Senses} practices. You will recognize activities that make sense and should not be changed. Then you'll find company practices that should be changed. If you are conscientious and careful, you may persuade your company's decision-makers to consider ways to modify company practices, by demonstrating the costs of not changing anything and getting the same results.

It's all about reducing costs, increasing profits, improving quality, and enhancing services. These are the wrappings for your gifts. But, be careful not to make waves; start with ripples. There will be lots of time later for the waves after you have proven yourself a worthy leader.

While analyzing the organization, you'll develop goals and plans to achieve those goals. You will learn how to measure the results. In this Stage, you'll learn how to make changes that actually work. You will build groups of employees that can work together to achieve objectives.

Earlier I wrote that this could be the most exciting or the most difficult time of your career. Learn to move slow and gradually build on your successes. People may think you are a rabble-rouser and oppose or interrupt your efforts. So, move cautiously. I'll show you some proven ways to improve your odds of success.

Here you'll find plenty of concepts to help you do it all: Insights like Constraints Management, RACI, TASTE, PAL, CSQ, EMPLOYEE TURNOVER, and DECISION-MAKING systems.

Assessing the Operation and Its People

Before moving to the next step in your career, take a moment to consider the secret ingredient of successful operations: a competent and committed workforce with a meaningful mission. Let's break this statement down.

QP67. How would you describe a competent workforce?

A competent workforce is a group of employees with both the skills and the desire to become workplace champions. Remember the lesson from my mom's bridge parties, where she discovered the championship ingredient within each of her friends and reinforced it every Saturday night. Remember Donald Laird's book SIZING UP PEOPLE where he told us that everyone has special qualities that set them apart from the common worker. I have found this to be true throughout my career. Many of my greatest successes would not have been possible without the special skills and knowledge of the workplace champions around me at the time.

The Ideal Employee

This exercise will help you identify worker qualities you desire the most. Draw a table with five columns labeled Name, Bad Traits, IDEAL TRAITS, Good Traits, and Name. In the first column, write the names of your worst employees. In the second column, write the bad things they do. In the last column, write the names of your best employees. In the second-to-last column write the good things they do. Now copy the Good Traits into the centre column under IDEAL TRAITS. Finally, copy the opposite of the Bad Traits into the center column under IDEAL TRAITS. Cut away everything but the center column and you have listed the traits of your IDEAL employee. This benchmark will help you in many ways: hiring, promoting, evaluating and encouraging the behavior of all your employees.

47

John Smithman

How to Determine the IDEAL Employee

NAMES	Bad Traits	IDEAL	Good Traits	NAMES

Figure 7: Determining the IDEAL employee traits

I conducted this exercise with 12 supervisors from a large manufacturing client (400 employees). After doing this exercise independently, they all had five characteristics in common. They wanted employees with **T.A.S.T.E.**: TIME savvy, positive ATTITUDE, appropriate job SKILLS, a TEAM player and someone who demonstrates EMPATHY for others. If you know what you want in an employee, you will find or develop it. Pay attention to what you want more of.

Here are the elements of TASTE defined by the IDEAL employee exercise.

TIME savvy

The employee has a good system to effectively apply their time. In Managing the Obvious (1994), Charles A. Coonradt related a story about Charles Percy, past CEO of Bell and Howell and later a United States Senator, who was asked by a reporter how he became company CEO at the age of 29. He replied, "I just follow the accepted rules of time management:

ITEMIZE. I list the results I want and the tasks required to achieve them.

CATEGORIZE. I put similar items together.

PRIORITIZE. I decide what things are most important and which ones can be put aside for later.

DELEGATE or ELIMINATE. I decide on what can better be done better by someone else and, more importantly, what doesn't have to be done at all."

Then, I delegate or eliminate everything.

As he worked his way up through the ranks of Bell and Howell, at each new position, he assigned ALL his work. Later, when the company was looking for someone to take on a new position, someone would say, "Let's give it to Percy because he has nothing to do!" All the way to the top office!

ATTITUDE

A positive attitude can be acquired if you adopt the practice of looking for the potential benefits in everything that happens. Replace the negative words you are tempted to use to describe a situation with positive ones. Words have the power to steer your thoughts and emotions. For example, when things go wrong, it is so hard not to feel "frustrated" and challenged. Yet, change the word to "fascinated" and your thoughts will turn to the opportunities. The words in your thoughts will change your focus from problem to potential.

SKILL

Job-related skills, yes, but also think skill-related jobs. We hire people with the skills to do the vacant job, but employees have personal skills that they bring with them to the job. Be aware that these new skills can create opportunities for you as you design or redesign jobs. It is good practice to match skills with jobs AND jobs with skills.

TEAMWORK

An employee that cannot only work well with others, but also can enhance the capability of the whole group through motivation and collaboration, is a valuable company asset.

EMPATHY

This is the ability to see things through another's eyes, being able to understand the feelings and thoughts of others. Empathy provides the secret ingredient that enables a leader to negotiate agreements and build consensus with others.

Employee Turnover

QP68. How would you describe a committed workforce?

When it is difficult to readily describe something, try describing its opposite. The common scourge of large companies, *Employee Turnover*, is a clear sign of uncommitted workers. New recruits are motivated and eager to learn their new skills until they become highly productive champions in the workplace. Through time however they lose interest and fade until they begin to drag their feet and become de-motivated. Then, they are fired or leave on their own accord.

Avoid Employee Turnover. Achieve commitment by promoting continuous self-improvement through progressive applied learning and compatible job assignments.

INTERVENTION TRAINING

Most training de-motivates. Training becomes available and employees are sent for various reasons. But the results are the Horizon Effect: the learning drains away soon after the employees return to work: TRAIN, then DRAIN. The course is a quick information dump. Within days, the information is lost.

Here are the challenges with most one-time training courses:

- Information is not absorbed (too much at once) and not supported when they return to work ("We don't do it that way here!");

- Training is reactive rather than proactive. Employees are sent just to fill the seats or spend the budget;
- The impact fades fast. Soon, things return to the way they were;
- It is very expensive: because of the small returns on investment;
- Performance goes up, then down; no standards are set, with little, if any, long term growth;
- People feel punished by 'remedial' training, rather than rewarded by 'developmental' training;
- There is no reinforcement during the 'practice' period (after the training);
- Because training is a one-time affair, there is little or no commitment from participants;
- Intermittent training doesn't foster steady professional growth; and
- The company investment is lost. It may even have a detrimental effect.

Progressive Applied Learning (PAL)

Training is applied over a period of time, with each new training session building on former ones to foster absorption of the material and ongoing improvement. Here are the benefits of progressive applied learning programs:

- Best return on the training investment
- Long-term gain and continuous improvement
- Once the ball is rolling, building momentum is easier
- Employees feel valued, not punished. Training is viewed as 'reward' and demonstrates confidence, as a promise of future growth opportunities
- Employee loyalty builds because they are growing professionally within the company
- Each topic or theme builds upon previous topics for continuous development
- Each new training application is shorter, cheaper, and more effective
- The company's investment is protected

Employees who are dedicated to continuous self-improvement in the pursuit of their goals are major ingredients to company success. A committed workforce is loyal, dedicated and supports the company mission.

QP69. What is a meaningful mission for the organization?

While it is not your role to define the company's mission, it is your responsibility to lead your operation in support of it. You must be able to describe it clearly for your employees and show them how their work supports it.

Good time management is described as ensuring that what you are doing right now is moving you toward your personal or organizational goals. The same can be said for the activities of the whole company. Is what you are doing right now moving you toward the company's mission?

Let's describe a meaningful mission statement.

A good Mission Statement is a direction, not a destination. It contains something for everyone in the organization. There are elements that draw the support of every member of the organization, from owners and shareholders, through managers, supervisors and frontline workers, to the customers. Yes, customers play a major role in a company's pursuit of its mission. Therefore, a Mission Statement is also a commitment.

QP70. What does high employee turnover tell you about a company?

Companies are known by the people they keep. Of all the resources a company has, only people have the ability to redesign themselves on the go. As a supervisor, you can allow these changes to happen at random or you can lead them.

The first signs of trouble are discontented employees. A sense of tension and nervousness prevails, as people lose interest and become paralyzed by indecision or start looking for work elsewhere. Productivity falls as people quit their jobs. Or worse yet, they stay on the job, but just quit working. A climbing turnover rate is deadly to a company. So let's have a look at how to avoid employee turnover.

First, what is turnover? Turnover is employees leaving and being replaced in a company. Employees quit or are fired and new employees hired. A little bit of turnover is healthy. New employees bring new ideas and skills. However, companies need continuity in their workers to benefit from their training and experience.

IN> WIN> POUT> OUT>

(company costs and benefits during the life of an employee)

The value of new employees is in their potential. Upon hiring, they are highly motivated, but not yet trained to produce. The hiring costs are recruiting, interviewing and testing, reference checks, tools, uniforms, passes, training, indoctrination, desk or office, fitting into the job, mistakes while learning. Hiring a new employee is extremely expensive. Associated is the huge cost of removing your best workers from the production line so they can train the new employees.

New employees don't begin to return value until six months or more after their hire. This is when they become the *workplace champion*: a fully trained and motivated, highly productive employee. The duration of this high productivity WIN stage depends on their training, supervision and working conditions.

In most companies, productivity begins to wane within a year or two as the employee loses interest. Now they are a fully-trained, but de-motivated, employee. And you are beginning to build a case file for replacing them. The cost of keeping the employee is growing.

I call these four stages in the life of an employee: IN>WIN> POUT>OUT>. The only stage without costs is the WIN stage. I will show you how to keep employees at this stage of their working life with your company.

As supervisor, don't look for the signs of turnover, work to avoid turnover altogether.

Study and practice employee MOTIVATION.

QP71. How do you motivate an employee?

Studies confirm that motivated workers are more productive, stay longer and provide better customer care. There are two kinds of motivation: external and internal. External motivation is reward or fear-based. External motivation works short-term only and can help get you started. Learn the key to internal motivation and you will see continuous development. Internal motivation comes from an internal urge to satisfy personal needs. The key then is to help an employee to see how their performance will help to fill their personal needs.

In Stage 1, you asked about your employees needs. Look at your notes. Are there needs that are still unfulfilled? Is there a way that you can help? You provide the key to open the door. There lies the specific answer to Question 71. Link each task or project to an employee's internally-driven urge to satisfy their specific needs.

Basic Human Needs

Underscoring specific needs, there are BASIC HUMAN NEEDS. My description is based on the work of Dr. William Glasser, author of Reality Therapy (1965) and Choice Theory (1998). *Survival*: the need for food, security, air; *Enjoyment*: the need for fun; *Power*: the need to control; *Belonging*: the need to associate; and *Freedom*: the need for choice. The theory is that all behavior can be explained by our continuous efforts to satisfy these needs. We will return to this Insight into human behavior again and again. It is basic to my understanding of how to explain workplace behavior, as taught to me by my colleague and former Glasser student, Shelley Brierley, M.Ed.

Next is a diagram to illustrate my understanding of how a company can help employees meet their basic human needs.

Human Needs

Figure 8: Meeting Human Needs in the Workplace

Figure 9: Blaise Pascal

We are usually more easily convinced by reasons we have found ourselves than by those which have occurred to others. - Blaise Pascal, Pensées (1670)

QP72. How do you improve the impact of training?

Many companies view training as an expense, because they are not good at assessing the value of training. As you can see in the Human Needs diagram (Figure 8), training plays a role in helping employees meet every basic need. The problem is often in the method of delivery. The proper application of training requires more space than I have here to cover it. I make a few observations about terminology, the "train-drain" principle, and progressive applied learning (PAL).

The word training itself is misleading. It implies that training is imparted to the student, as in "training a dog". In fact, the greatest amount of learning is through self-training. The value of learning is in its ability to help us meet our personal goals and satisfy our human needs. Training therefore should be self-motivated.

Train-Drain - The Horizon Effect

Companies tend to arrange training in big bites, by designing full-day or full-week training courses. A vast amount of knowledge or skill is delivered in a short amount of time. This method overloads the student ("the cup overflows"), leading to fast drainage of the knowledge. Train, then drain: as knowledge is quickly forgotten over the following few days. Training like this is like an athlete trying to build his muscles too quickly, without giving time for the body to adjust. It can cause damage.

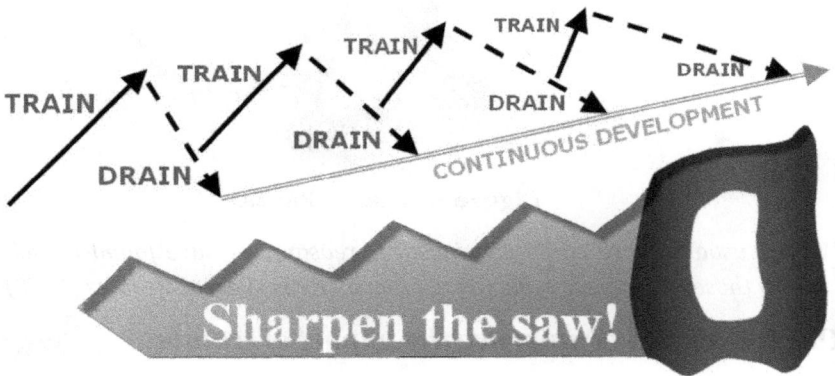

Figure 10: Continuous Development through Periodic Training

Training should be done in small applications over a longer period of time to allow time for the brain to assimilate and the body to practice the new knowledge. This better training method is called progressive applied learning.

Fine Tuning Performance

As the employee supervisor, your role is to develop their natural skills to improve performance for results. You are really a coach to your workplace champion team.

QP73. How do you track your worker's performance against their short and long term goals?

During your weekly 1:1s, regularly review the employee's performance against their goals. Start and end each meeting with a reference to a goal. Look for elements of current performance that plug into goals and give proper recognition for it. Here's a story to illustrate how trivial recognition can have substantial impact.

John's Story

While learning to supervise, I took every chance to learn to do my job better and easier. I attended a management course where the instructor told us how Hewlett Packard's 'golden banana' award was born. A manager was looking for a way to appreciate an employee's performance, when he spotted a banana on his desk that was left over from lunch. He knew the importance of good timing and the time for a reward was now, so he presented the banana in a ceremonial way to his worker and praised him for a job well done. I thought the story was cute, but I didn't think that I had paid much attention to it until one day I was in a similar situation.

My security systems supervisor was standing in front of my desk beaming with self-satisfaction after telling me about a challenge he had just resolved. I knew intuitively that this was the right time for a 'banana' award. I didn't have a banana, but I did have a gold star sticker in my desk drawer. So, on a whim, I ceremoniously gave John his gold star while I praised his ingenious solution to the challenge he had faced. We both laughed and I forgot about it in the days that followed.

However, about a year later while meeting John in our weekly 1:1 meeting, when I had just praised him for another job well done, he observed, with some mock sadness, that I had not given him any more gold stars since that first one a year ago. I smiled as I remembered the occasion.

Then, John took out his wallet and showed me the gold star that I had given him last year. It was stuck to his driver's license! He had kept it because it reminded him of a proud moment.

As a supportive supervisor, always look for moments like those to cement your relationships with your employees and anoint them with special rewards.

QP74. What is your training plan for each worker that reports to you?

As shown in the discussion about progressive applied learning, it is important to tie relevancy to training. That makes training worthwhile and relates it to self-motivated career development instead of a requirement of the job. There's no magic in doing "requirements of the job." But contributing to the formation of a future does hold significance.

Use some of your 1:1 times to talk about and plan training or other learning opportunities to contribute to the career growth of your employees. Encourage your employees to get involved in their own development. Training should be a positive response to their needs not a forced response to yours.

QP75. Which of your daily tasks can you assign to members of your work group?

Help them learn how to achieve your goals. Assigning a task to someone else helps them grow as they prove their abilities and it helps free you up for more challenging work. Earlier I suggested you share the leadership of your work group by rotating your group meeting's chair job. This is just the beginning of what else you can share with them.

QP76. Have you established a schedule for training members to assume these tasks?

Plan this development to coincide with meaningful dates or moments in their career, like the anniversary of their starting date. The more hooks you work into such assignments, the stronger their motivation to do it well.

QP77. Have you discussed ways to modify their jobs with equipment, tools or other resources?

Additional work assigned to your employees should be a challenge, but not a burden. In your position you can keep it palatable by providing equipment, tools or other help to ensure their success in taking it on.

Discipline... The Hard Decisions

QP78. How do you discipline a worker for poor performance?

Quickly, privately, and with empathy. Too many supervisors take notes and record bad behavior for some unknown reason, and then withhold any disciplinary action until a more comfortable time like during the annual employee evaluation. Or, they may use it as a reason to withhold a raise in pay.

You wouldn't treat a dog like that. Punish a dog for something he did several days earlier and he would just be confused and learn nothing from your scolding except that you are a bad person. Dog training is simple. Reward or punish as soon as possible after the behavior for best results. Instant feedback is the best teacher.

Praise publicly and scold privately is a common rule. Scolding privately is always a good policy because another's opinion of you is a strong motivator. However, praise publicly is not always the best choice. It depends on your employee (QB4, QB8). Some people don't want to be embarrassed by public praise. Others are thrilled by it. Know your employee. Know what's appropriate in each case.

59

QP79. Where do you discipline your worker? What environment factors are best?

Feedback has such a powerful influence on people. Be careful to ensure that you have all the right elements in place to take advantage of its power. When, where and how you give feedback is critical. Also, because of the potential reactions from employees these days when they have more avenues for retaliating against unfair supervisors, you must be careful. Withholding privileges may not be considered fair. Bestowing special rewards may not be legal. Many companies have rules around the allowed feedback mechanisms available to you. Check with your personnel or human resources office before disciplining or rewarding anyone. Learn what's appropriate in your environment. For example, as I write this, it is not appropriate in some companies for a man to discipline a woman behind closed doors.

QP80. Does another member of your organization's service team need to be involved?

Human Resources departments retain members whose role it is to offer support in incidents of discipline. Often it may depend on the level of discipline to determine who needs to be present when an employee is formally disciplined.

QP81. What is the proper process for engaging the employee union's participation?

Where there is a employee union present, there are usually negotiated agreements detailing how an employee is supervised; with levels of discipline based on repetition over time and job levels. Union agreements are designed to protect both the employee and management from improper practices. Each case is different, so be sure to check this out with respect to your organization.

Summary (Stage 3)

We have had a look at some pretty serious elements of a company's health, such as the challenge of employee turnover, the problem with maintaining the Status Quo, proper training processes, and discipline. You learned a proven time and career management method.

You heard my mom's principle of motivation by recognizing the values in people around you. You discovered the secret ingredients of a successful operation: a competent and committed workforce with a meaningful mission.

We talked about managing performance through thoughtful training, focused feedback and deliberate discipline, under company rules.

Next, in Stage 4: A Company of Champions, you'll consider answers to questions on Effective Change, Productive Teams and Sound Succession Planning: the secrets to long-term company growth.

John Smithman

Stage 4: A Company of Champions
build effective teams and efficient systems

TOPICS
The Champion Supervisor
Stan's Story
The Impact of Change
Planning Changes
Margaret's Story
Building Consensus
Building Strength through Teamwork
The Bridge Building Exercise
Decider - Promoter - Supporter - Analyzer
Systems... Effectiveness before Efficiency
Succession: Passing the Torch
Succession Planning: Costs and Benefits
Costs of Not Generating Successors
Tackling Time Loss - Making Time Work For You!

The Champion Supervisor

A workplace champion is someone who looks for and enhances championship behavior in themselves. The champion supervisor recognizes and rewards championship in others.

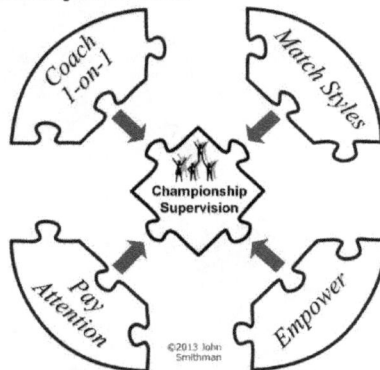

Figure 11: Championship Supervision

62

Stan's Story

This story from a champion manager shows the humanity and impact of his style of supervision. It illustrates the five C's of superior supervision: Communication, Consequence, Contrasting, Coaching and Creating the future.

The announcement: a significant new contract!

Paul, the general manager of a Canadian manufacturing plant, asked the employees to gather for some good news. It was supposed to be a happy occasion; but one of the employees – Stan – did his best to dampen the event. Slouching in his seat with one arm draped around the back of his chair, he said, "I suppose now we'll get to use the executive washroom, eh?"

Stan was known as a rabble-rouser at the plant. You could count on his negative attitude and putdowns of management.

Later, in the manager's office...

After the meeting, the general manager summoned Stan to his office:

"I suppose you're gonna fire me!?" Stan said belligerently.

Paul responded, "You think you're being funny and smart with your sarcastic re-marks; but you're not smart. Your friends aren't laughing with you, they are laughing at you. Yeah I could fire you; but you'd just go to another company and get fired there too in time; and the cycle continues; or you could break this cycle right now! With your intelligence, skill, and courage aimed at positive expression, you could become something of value: a lead hand in a couple of months; maybe even plant foreman in a couple of years! But you have to decide to change your focus."

The Rest of the Story...

It happened. A few months later, the general manager noticed that Stan was one of the volunteers for a weekend job that was optional. In a few months, he became a lead hand and eventually he did become plant foreman.

The Real Impact...

Years later, after he had left the company, Paul was invited back to a company Christmas Party for employees and their families. A lady came up to him and said, "Sir, you don't know me, but I am Stan's wife. I just wanted to thank you for not firing Stan that day. He is now a volunteer fireman in our community, a loving father to our two boys, and a wonderful husband. Thank you so much."

Wow! A volunteer fireman; two beloved children; and a grateful wife. Most managers have no idea of the wide-ranging impact they have when they properly supervise people at work.

No supervisor can anticipate the widespread impact of their decisions.

The Impact of Change

At some point in your development, you will want to make changes in your organization based on decisions you have made. So, how do you generate support for your decisions?

You must "see" the results clearly before you start. This will motivate you and others. And, you must acquire the resources for the change. It requires good planning to reduce the negative impacts of change.

Change is best when you have obtained a consensus of agreement amongst those most affected by the change. There is risk in change without proper preparation.

An analogy helps us grasp the impact of change.

A lizard's skin doesn't stretch. For a lizard to grow, it must shed its skin and expose the tender, vulnerable, new skin beneath. It must exercise caution as it climbs over rocks and twigs to prevent injury. Until its new skin toughens, a cut could cause it to bleed to death.

People are like lizards when it comes to change. To grow, they must shed their old habits as they adopt new ones. Wise supervisors exercise empathy and patience toward their employees as they gently begin to implement new ways of working.

Allow time to ease the transitions.

Planning Changes

QC82. How will your planned changes impact workers, workflow and working conditions?

Margaret's Story

One day the company's carpenters showed up in Margaret's office. They were tearing out the wall in front of her desk. She asked, "What are you doing?"

They said, "We're tearing out the wall to put in a new door."

She asked, "Why?"

They said, "Don't know."

That night, Margaret was awake all night worrying about what was happening at work. Had she been fired? Will she have to look for a new job? Why wasn't she warned about what was happening?

The next day, she worked up enough courage to meet with her boss. Highly stressed from her worrying, she was prepared to say, "I quit!"

Her supervisor asked Margaret not to worry, while she found out what was happening.

Later, Margaret learned that the carpenters were so efficient that they began work before the managers had time to notify her supervisor of the upcoming positive changes to their workplace.

Trust can be severely damaged from poor planning and poor communications.

QC83. What are the necessary ingredients of effective change?

*THE FIVE COMPONENTS OF CHANGE

> Without VISION there is Confusion
>
> Without INCENTIVE there is Resistance
>
> Without SKILLS there is Anxiety
>
> Without RESOURCES there is Frustration
>
> Without a PLAN there is a Treadmill

*source: Caroline Rowan, Results-Centred Leadership

Building Consensus

The next two questions address the main steps for effecting change: decision-making and consensus-building. In autocratic organizations, the approach may be boss decides, employees obey. However, I've learned that it is much easier if you spend the time and effort to build consensus before you start.

QC84. What is your process for making rational decisions?

Implementing large projects affects more people. If you want these people to support the project, understand the logic and reasons behind the changes.

I use a weighted decision matrix to weigh the pros and cons of a decision because it documents the process and gives me selling points to use later when I am building consensus. Here is how it works.

Step 1: Identify the criteria and develop the weights. Here's an example for a company considering which of three new services to offer its customers. To demonstrate the process I have selected five criteria: Profit Margin, Skills Needed, Capital Investment, Easy to sell, and Easy to deliver. To begin, I compare each criterion to each of the others and decide which is the more important of the two. I write the winner's letter in the cell. I prioritize them by largest number of winners and write the total number of A's, B's, etc in the Wgt. column

Develop *Criteria* Priorities and Weightings

	Criteria	B	C	D	E	Priorities	Wgt.
A	Profit Margin	a	c	a	a	A	3
B	Skills Needed		b	b	b	B	3
C	Capital Investment			c	c	C	2
D	Easy to sell				d	D	1

Figure 12: Priority Criteria Weightings

The Decision-Making Matrix

CUSTOMER SERVICE DECISIONS

C h o i c e s

Criteria	Wt.	Service 1	Service 2	Service 3
Profit Margin	3	x 2 = 6	x 1 = 3	x 3 = 9
Skills Needed	3	x 1 = 3	x 2 = 6	x 3 = 9
Capital Investment	2	x 3 = 6	x 1 = 2	x 2 = 4
Easy to sell	1	x 3 = 3	x 2 = 2	x 1 = 1
TOTALS =>		18	13	23

Weighting	X	Rating	=	Score

Figure 13: Decision-Making Matrix

Step 2: I write the weights in the Wgt. column and the ratings of each service against each criterion. Multiply and write the score under each Service column. When I total the scores, I see that Service 3 is the best choice to implement.

Making decisions is both important and difficult. Make choices that all stakeholders have confidence in, and that are somehow justifiable. Document decisions in structured ways to ensure that others will be able to see your reasons for making a decision, long after the choice is made.

There are often many different criteria that need to be considered in making a decision. It is essential to identify the criteria, and to evaluate the choice with respect to those criteria as precisely as possible.

A decision-making matrix is a simple tool that can be very useful in making complex decisions, especially in cases where there are many choices and many criteria to be considered. I now have a record documenting how I arrived at my decision.

I have found this decision-making process useful at union grievance hearings for explaining how I made job-filling choices, without just picking the most senior union applicant.

QC85. How do you obtain change consensus from stakeholders?

If you want people to support a major change, design a feature or function into each project that answers the needs or concerns of each stakeholder. Put a little something into the project for everyone and you will minimize any challenges or roadblocks. By doing this you are adding winners to the completed project. The more winners, the more likely the project will complete.

Start your planning by meeting privately with a representative from each stake-holder group, state your intention and ask for their inputs into your project plan. Then modify your plan to address the needs they express. Or, if you can't give them what they need, negotiate a compromise.

Henry Kissinger was famous for getting decisions approved through negotiation. Learn the interests of each group and look for overlaps between their circles of interest. Those overlaps are the beginnings of consensus. If you ask enough of the right questions you will build these areas of overlap to where you may even achieve complete consensus and gain the full support you need. Plan your projects to please the most people.

CONSENSUS is based on finding the agreeables!

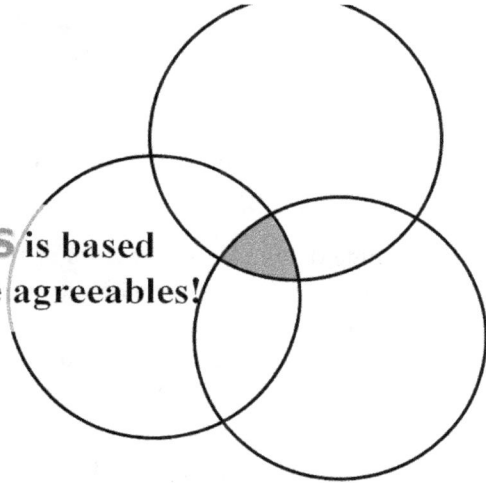

Figure 14: Building Consensus

The rings represent the areas of need and desire of each party. The deeper you research these issues, the better chance you will have for finding the agreeables. And the closer you examine them, the closer you'll get to CONSENSUS and SYNERGY.

Building Strength through Teamwork

CEOs dream of highly-effective teams and efficient systems to help their companies grow. Bigger organizations can serve more people and gain more wealth for their owners and shareholders. If you can build highly-effective teams and efficient systems, you will become very valuable to your organization.

Highly effective teams take advantage of SYNERGY.

QC86. What is team synergy?

Synergy can be explained by an old story about a horse pull at a county fair (much like the tractor pulls of today). One year, the winner pulled 4,500 pounds. The runner-up pulled 4,400 pounds. Both horses performed so well that folks wondered what the two horses might pull if they worked together. So they yoked the two horses together and the horses pulled more than 12,000 pounds. This increase of 33% over individual effort is the essence of synergy.

With people synergy can be much greater because factors other than muscle and leverage affect the results. All companies strive for synergy, but few really put the effort into properly yoking the team together. Unlike horses, people realize synergy through communication, commitment, trust, vision, leadership, followership, and understanding.

QC87. How do you build an effective team?

First, we determine the nature of the tasks needed to complete the project. A team is people working together with a common purpose. They must be matched to the tasks. But more than just having appropriate job skills, team members need the skills of communication, collaboration and creativity to achieve synergy.

If their behavior styles are compatible, team members will be more comfortable in their collaboration. Recall that the four primary team styles are the Deciders, the Promoters, the Supporters and the Analyzers. Teams should have members representing each of these style traits, because every trait offers special benefits.

The Bridge Building Exercise

Here is a story to illustrate how each behavior style contributed their strengths in a team whose purpose was to build a bridge across a creek with some ropes and boards in a limited time period.

The team leader explained the purpose to the team members, who immediately sprung into action, each in his own way. The Deciders told the Supporters what to do; while the Analyzers organized, counted and measured the materials to be used. The Promoters acted as cheerleaders.

When the bridge was completed, the first one to cross the bridge to the other side was a Promoter with hands held high in triumph while the Analysers recorded their use of the resources (time and materials), for the record.

QC88. What are the 3 basic functions of the team leader?

To describe the team's purpose;

To provide the resources needed; and

To encourage, oversee and recognize achievements.

QC89. What team roles are assigned to team members?

The ADMINISTRATOR role is similar to that of a group supervisor, who assigns work, oversees and motivates team members. Usually taken by team leader, it may be assigned to another member. The PUBLICIST communicates the team's actions and achievements to the rest of the organization. The AUDITOR records the activities and tracks the resources as they are consumed by team activities.

QC90. How do you assess your team's working style?

Create a Team Style chart and mark your team member's names on the chart in positions where they seem to fit. It will become quickly obvious where there are opportunities to add or remove people to balance the team's style.

The following chart clearly presents the behavior styles of the members of a board of volunteer directors who guide the operations of a local non-profit organization. The style map quickly explained an identified weakness in their ability to record and report their activities to their organization's sponsors.

Decider - Promoter - Supporter - Analyzer

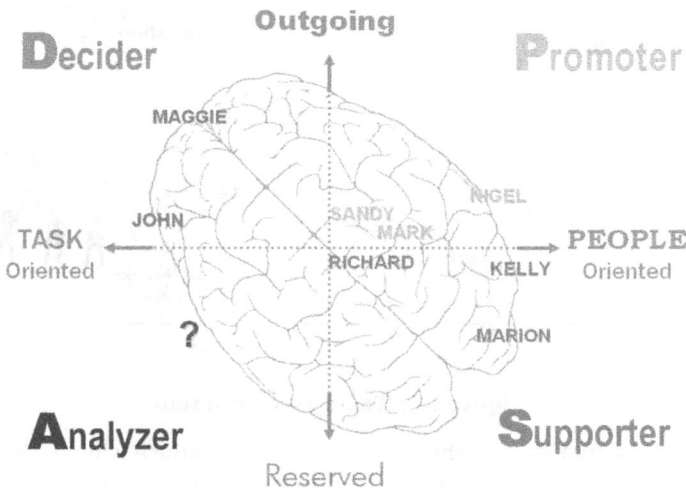

Figure 15: Team Working Styles

71

As volunteers, they worked at what they wanted to work on, not necessarily what the organization needed. I encouraged them to recruit a new board member with demonstrated Analyzer strengths.

QC91. What are the 5 Stages of Team Development?

Teams go through stages as they develop towards optimum performance. At the CREATION stage, they are excited, curious and motivated. As time goes by, they enter a CONFLICT stage where they begin to compete for the attention of the team leader. Distrust may set in. Then, as they begin to see the values and strengths of other team members, they enter the CONNECTION stage and become mutually supportive. The COLLABORATION stage is when they regain sight of their team's purpose and start to make good progress as they cooperate to achieve their goals. The final stage is CELEBRATION, a time to rejoice with pride on a job well done.

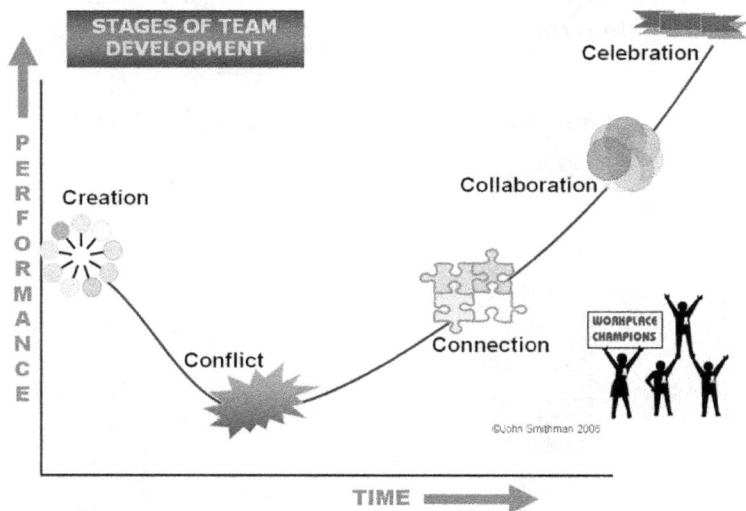

Figure 16: Team Development

There are two stages where the risk of team failure is high: the Conflict and the Connection stages. At the Conflict stage, members become critical of the short-comings of their teammates. Arguments break out. The Leader sees this discord, fears that it will only get worse and considers disbanding the team. However, if the leader can just be patient and let the members work out their own differences, this stage will resolve itself, as members begin to make CONNECTIONS and see the potential in combining their individual strengths.

If we refer to the Conflict stage as the War Zone, we can refer to the Connection stage as Love City. Performance wanes in these stages as members are distracted by their emotions. The leader must work to return their focus on team purpose.

Systems... Effectiveness before Efficiency

QC92. How does your operation contribute to organization workflow?

Think of your work as a link in the process chain from receiving people and supplies to modifying and delivering them to consumers. In a well organized operation, work flows smoothly, with no hiccups. You can identify interruptions in workflow by the changes in performance at transition points. Like three lanes of traffic merging into one lane, work can slow down at company bottlenecks.

Dr. Eliahu Goldratt's excellent book, The Goal (1988) reveals a story about a plant experiencing bottlenecks in their production chain. Losses in productivity occur when materials are sitting idle at a machine that others are using for example. In his book, Dr. Goldratt explains through his Theory of Constraints how to identify and resolve these workplace constraints by cause and effect analysis.

QC93. How can you measure and enhance the effectiveness of your link in the process chain?

Consult with your boss and your workers on the effectiveness of your group's contribution to the company mission. There are many ways to measure productivity. For example, you may establish a checker to monitor your production as meeting or exceeding a number of products per hour. You could report on the quality of your work in terms of damage, tests passed or failures found and consumer feedback. Are your machine bottlenecks because of their age or obsolescence? Develop feedback systems for your employees. Consider having them monitor their own performance. Will a new machine remove the constraints to your productivity? When were your work systems installed, last reviewed or modified? Are your people in good health and properly trained for their work? Do they have the authority to change the system on the spot if needed or do they have to get permission from a manager who may be away for the day?

QC94. What needs to change and why?

Constraints, People, Equipment, Sales and Service management are areas where you may find opportunities for growth or fine-tuning. Training can be motivational. Use your decision matrix tool to choose the right actions to take in your workplace. Before implementing anything new, prepare a change plan that notifies the people affected by the change. Give them lots of notice so that they have time to adjust. Remember the Lizard story and give your employees time and training to help them shed their old skins and replace old habits with new ones.

Consult with others who may be affected by your changes, before you make them. No one likes surprises. Vow to give no surprises to your colleagues. Share your thoughts beforehand and allow for feedback before taking action. Build that consensus we talked about earlier (QC85). This will protect them and it will help you progress more smoothly. It is time well spent.

Succession: Passing the Torch.

CEOs dream of succession when they can pursue their own dreams by passing the torch to their rising workplace champions like you.

QC95. What are the costs and benefits of succession planning?

Succession planning creates succession-minded managers who develop workplace champions to eventually replace their own jobs.

Succession Planning: Costs and Benefits

Productivity initially wanes, and then explodes. Training investment is moderate, but small compared to future revenues. Productivity grows. There will be more customers and repeat sales, leading to greater shareholder profits.

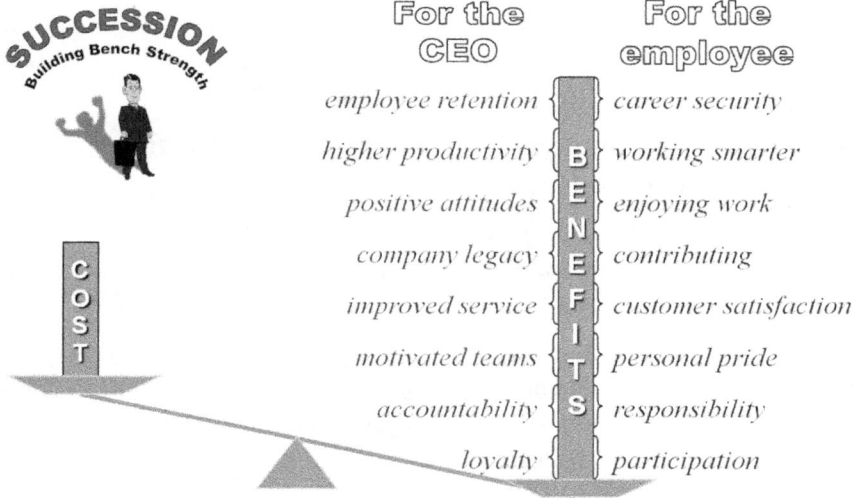

Figure 17: Succession Benefits

Costs of Not Generating Successors

Good employees see few opportunities and leave the company; managers retire 'on the job'; non-sharing managers take their knowledge and skills with them when they go; productivity improvements are unlikely; excitement and energy is gone.

QC96. What changes are needed in your operation to support succession?

Establish the method of progressive applied learning to build the know-how of workplace champions.

Increase delegation, with responsibility AND authority, to all employees.

Build highly-effective, high-performance teams where workers learn responsibility and self-leadership

QC97. What is your succession plan for replacing yourself?

Review your champion logbooks. Have you found some dormant champions around you? Have you been keeping notes on their abilities, hopes and progress?

You may even have had opportunities over the past few months to allow them to extend their talents. Who have you been grooming to take over your responsibilities? Who are your champions?

QC98. How can you accept more responsibility to free up your own boss to achieve his goals?

The best way to become very valuable to your organization is to be able to do your own tasks effectively and still have time to help your colleagues (QB5,QB9) and boss (QB10) with theirs.

Remember the points made in the answers to QB24, QB29 to QB32, where you heard of the challenges being faced by your boss in the pursuit of his goals. Use that information now that you have learned how to effectively supervise your people and lead your teams.

Tackling Time Loss - Making Time Work For You!

Giving only random attention to what must be done each day is time theft.

QC99. How can you work more effectively on your job?

Control time and see dramatic improvements in both effectiveness and efficiency.

List tasks to be done, with values and deadlines to meet. Add the resource costs for each task. Prioritize the tasks and do in priority sequence.

Close your office door at a scheduled time each day to manage your task list.

Batch tasks and communications and do them more efficiently in batches.

Schedule regular meetings with employees to allow time-saving here, too.

If you have long-term goals that require actions over several days or weeks, break the activity up into small pieces that can be done in short bursts of activity. Use the Daily Effectiveness Chart to whittle away at long-term projects.

Name _____   Week Ending _____

Daily Effectiveness Check (DEC)

My two most important accomplishments this week were:

1. _____

2. _____

Effectiveness Check: In the areas to the left, identify five key areas of Effectiveness that are especially important to you. Rate yourself on a scale of one to ten each day as to your performance level in each area.

AREA DAY	MON	TUE	WED	THU	FRI	SAT	SUN	TOTAL
1.								
2.								
3.								
4.								
5.								
TOTAL								

Last Week's Average	This Week's Avg. (Box A)/35	Box A

Areas that require more focus and effort:

_____

_____

Goals for next week (Consider both professional and personal short-term goals.):

_____

_____

_____

_____

Figure 18: The Daily Effectiveness Checkup

Use the following goal-setting chart weekly to achieve significant results.

John Smithman

At the end of each week, write down two personal goals and two professional goals to achieve next week. Then, at the end of the week, check your progress and finish entering the details.

Using this chart invokes your mind's focusing power to the degree that, even though you may not even look at this chart again during the week, you may discover that these goals were achieved by you subconsciously!

Goal Setting

NAME_____   DATE_____

List both personal and professional goals. Then, prioritize how you wish to achieve them. Indicate if the goal is a paradigm-change for you. Finally, list your deadline to achieve, and dollar value involved.

Priority	Personal Goals	Paradigm-Change: Yes or No	Deadline	Date Achieved	Dollar Value

Priority	Professional Goals	Paradigm-Change: Yes or No	Deadline	Date Achieved	Dollar Value

Figure 19: Weekly Goal Setting Form

Summary (Stage 4)

Effective change, productive teams and sound succession planning are the secrets to long-term company growth

In this Stage of your growth as a developmental supervisor and workplace champion, you considered how to build your own operation and ultimately your entire organization to become a Company of Champions. To become a champion company among companies:

You saw how to make decisions that stick because they are well-planned and supported by stakeholders.

You saw how to build consensus to guarantee success for your projects

You saw how to analyze operational workflow effectiveness.

You saw how to become more efficient in your effectiveness.

You saw the components of effective change.

You built productive teams where every member has a significant role.

You saw the importance of developing job skills with self-image to move successfully up the management ladder.

You saw the secrets of long term growth through high performance, self-led teams and developmental supervision.

You will ensure that everyone in the organization is a workplace champion with a significant role to play and a long term plan for professional growth in pursuit of company mission.

Stage 5: More Support
learning never ends

TOPICS

Behavior
Five Human Needs
Self-Motivation
Fear
Mind Influence
Mantra
Motivation
Rita's Story
Suggested Reading
Insights, Quotations, Rules, Champion Stories
Testimonials

As we review these 99 Questions, we have followed a track that took us from first observations to ongoing improvements.

To support our workers and colleagues through this development, we'll conduct ourselves with empathy and respect. Here are some people considerations.

Behavior

People don't do things for the wrong reasons; people do things for their reasons.

When questioning employee behavior that seems illogical or unexpected, use your empathy and reason to guess what need or purpose is met by this behavior.

This practice will give you new perspectives to help if you decide to question the employee's motivations. Your perspective may help to build your trust levels as well, when you show that you are considering your employee's perspective and needs before taking action.

Five Human Needs

Survival - basic needs: water, food, air, clothing, security

Fun - enjoyment, pleasure

Power - control, management

Belonging - friendship, association, love

Freedom - freedom of choice

Shelley Brierley of Oasis Consulting taught me that humans have five needs that must be met for them to feel balanced. We do whatever it takes to meet the needs continuously: in a open, clean and fair way; or in a closed, dirty and unfair way. To keep our five need tanks full at all times, we do whatever it takes.

Sometimes our drive interferes with another's needs and a conflict arises. For example, a man may have a job where he feels that his need for power is not being met. He goes home after work each day and beats his dog or frightens his wife to meet his need for control. This is his way of getting his power need met at the expense of another.

To help resolve this conflict, encourage this person to replace his negative actions with positive ones that will serve the same need. For our example, another activity might be to join a club and run for a position of power on the executive board. Or take up a hobby, like woodworking, to feed that Power need for control.

Self-Motivation

They say that self-motivation is the best motivation because it is based on the self-fulfilment of internal human needs. If you manage someone at work who behaves in a strange way, one way to resolve the problem is to consider which of the human needs is being met by the behavior. Then, suggest a different behavior for the worker. If the different behavior is a positive one, the worker is very likely to drop the old behavior.

Fear

There are only four psychological fears that can stop us in our tracks.

Fear of **FAILURE** can de-motivate us from taking risks.

Fear of **EMBARASSMENT** holds us back from public actions.

Fear of **ACHIEVEMENT** and the responsibilities that success holds may also scare us away from realizing our potential.

Fear of **REJECTION** prevents us from taking actions with people.

Mind Influence

The theory is that our minds have two patterns of thinking: the Left Brain deals with rational thinking like the relationships between numbers and mathematics, counting and goal setting, and the Right Brain deals with irrational thinking like the influence of art and music that touches our hearts and certain feelings like joy and empathy that make us human.

We should use our whole mind to see the big picture and allow all our perceptions to jointly motivate our thoughts and actions.

The Championship Style Map attempts to locate the mind source for our behaviors in its analysis. You can see an image of the brain superimposed on the preferred behavior matrix.

Mantra

Nothing Grows in the Soil of Despair

This mantra emerged from my subconscious to help me through a depressing time of my career when one of my business partners made a huge mistake that precipitated a $1 million lawsuit which was threatening to destroy my work life. She ran away and left me holding the bag. I had another business at the time that was beginning to suffer from my distractions with the lawsuit.

I lied awake nights feeling sorry for myself, feeling like an innocent victim. In the middle of the night, one night, I realized that if I allowed this worry to take over my thoughts, my other business would fail too. So I developed a mantra to remind me what was important right now. I realized that wounds heal with time and it's important not to let the trivial present interrupt my long term future. Soon, this too will pass and life will move on.

Nothing grows in the soil of despair became my mantra, my constant reminder whenever I felt pulled into victim thinking. It refocused my attention from the down dips back to the up ticks of my business track.

Negative thought is an unhealthy environment for positive results. My new mantra helped me flip the switch from negative to positive. I found opportunities where before I saw nothing but challenge. And the right lawyer helped me get my life back onto the upward slope.

It's good practice to think through a challenge and develop a solution that can be paraphrased in our minds as a memorable, short statement. The statement becomes a mantra to reset our thoughts when logical thinking becomes difficult.

We are composed of both our emotional and our rational thoughts. They work together to motivate us. But, in a one-on-one battle, I believe that emotion wins. Anything that can stabilize our emotion when the panic sets in is a good thing... because Nothing Good Grows in the Soil of Despair.

Motivation

Internal motivation is stronger and more enduring than external motivation. Punish someone for not behaving the way you want and you will motivate them to act quickly. Linking their actions to their own personal goals may take a bit longer, but this motivation endures. Study your workers, uncover what motivates them internally and you'll have one secret for success as a people manager.

Summary (Stage 5)

This is a good time for developmental supervision in the workplace, a good time for the workplace champion builder. Our companies have suffered too long from neglect. Employee turnover is rampant in large companies.

You have begun to make your mark as the new supervisor. People are watching you. There are certain things that you'll be expected to do. There will be certain things that your boss won't expect. Be persistent, but courteous. Sometimes bosses need a little prompting.

Rita's Story

I can't remember when I first met Rita. She was just there... with a spray bottle and a dust-rag in her hands for keeping our office desks and countertops clean and fresh.

Rita was a slight woman, about 5'5", with silver hair and a soft Scottish accent. At the time, I was office supervisor in The University of British Columbia's parking and security office and Rita was assigned to clean our offices by the university's maintenance services department.

One day, while dusting my desk, she quietly asked if the recent Patrol vacancy had been filled. I said that I didn't think that my boss, the Director, had decided on anyone yet. After a few seconds, and assuming that she had a son or nephew who was applying for the security patrol job, I said, "Why do you ask?"

Rita replied that she had sent in an application. I said, "For whom?" And she said that this was her 5th application for the job and that she wondered if she had any chance of getting it. I quickly corrected my assumptions, and muttered something about sometimes you have to ask many times to get the thing you want; and carried on with my work.

But I couldn't get Rita out of my mind. I support the principle of giving jobs to those who really want them, in spite of their apparent shortcomings. I believe that people can surprise you with their talents. So, one day while visiting with my boss in his office, I was ready with an answer when he remarked, "Can you believe that Rita, she's applied for a patrol job five times over the past few years?"

I commented, "She certainly is persistent and she does a very good job of cleaning our offices. Why don't you give her a chance?"

Rita received the patrol job that year. Not only that; but she immediately began to earn credits. She was sincere, honest, highly ethical, and she took the teasing from her male counterparts well. She soon earned a promotion to team supervisor. She had gained the respect of both the security manager and other patrol members.

Until now, I was watching from a distance as I managed the parking department. But my fortunes were also about to change.

The Parking and Security department director left the University and the Vice President began searching for his replacement.

Meanwhile, he asked me to fill in as acting director. After seven months of searching for a qualified ex-policeman to take the job, he recognized my performance by promoting me to the post of director of both departments.

That was when Rita entered the picture again.

The Patrol Manager retired. First, I promoted the most senior, qualified supervisor. It wasn't long before he realized he wasn't up to the task, and asked to have his old job back. So, I took a risk. I skipped the other candidates and gave Rita a chance. It wasn't just because I admired her perseverance. She had everything I needed in a Security Manager: ethics, drive, determination, courage and vision.

I remember one day hearing one of Rita's team members giving her a hard time in the hallway. I listened closely. He was objecting to a task that she had assigned to him; and he was at least 100 pounds heavier and eight inches taller than she. He had just said, "And if I don't do it, what are YOU going to do about it?"

Rita waited a few seconds while the echo of his defiance died down. Then she replied with a quiet strength, "You just don't do it and you will find out what I will do about it."

I asked her later, wasn't she nervous speaking up to him like that. And she said "A little." So I asked how she learned her great management skills. She replied curtly, "I have four grown children, Mr. Smithman."

Rita was a great security manager:

She increased the proportion of women in the security force. Women patrollers brought a whole new perspective and dimension to the university security force at a time when it was sorely needed.

She introduced bike patrols, which was a new thing at the time. Only one other security force in Canada had bike patrols – the Vancouver Police department.

She introduced Rape Aggression Defense training to teach campus women how to defend themselves if attacked.

She managed the security group through an ugly month-long strike in 1992.

Rita inspired all who met her.

What are the lessons we can learn from this true story?

- Perseverance Pays
- High Ethics and Strength of Character wins
- Strength of Character trumps Physical Strength
- Talents are Not Always Clearly Visible
- Leadership is the Ability to See and Reward Talents
- Progress is Not Without Risk
- Ask For What You Want

Rita, the cleaning lady, revolutionized security services at UBC. I will always re-member her strength of character and her dedication to duty. Rita was an inspiration with her wee, quiet voice and her huge potential.

Workplace champions are all around you. Look for them, release their power!

Be a champion in your workplace;
learn, listen, and pay attention to
the behaviors and performance
that you want more of:
from others and from yourself.

John Smithman
Vancouver, Canada
October 2013

Suggested Reading

The following people are my mentors. Although I've not met most of them, nevertheless, they have guided my growth as a workplace champion.

I owe my successes to Captain Henry Robert, James Allen, Evelyn King Smithman, Peter Drucker, Donald and Eleanor Laird, Shelley Brierley, Eliahu Goldratt, Charles Coonradt, Donald O. Clifton, Paula Nelson, Michael Gerber, Mike and Diane Larkin, and Roger C Parker.

The writers of these books are my Workplace Champions!

ROBERT'S RULES of ORDER, Henry M. Robert (1876)

AS A MAN THINKETH, James Allen (1901)

THE PRACTICE OF MANAGEMENT, Peter Drucker (1954)

SIZING UP PEOPLE, Donald and Eleanor Laird (1964)

THE GOAL, Eliahu Goldratt (1984)

THE GAME OF WORK, Charles Coonradt (1984)

LOOKING GOOD IN PRINT, Roger C Parker (1988)

IT'S NOT LUCK!, Eliahu Goldratt (1994)

SOAR WITH YOUR STRENGTHS, Donald O Clifton, Paula Nelson (1995)

THE E-MYTH REVISITED, Michael Gerber (1995)

MANAGING THE OBVIOUS, Charles Coonradt (1997)

THEORY OF CONSTRAINTS, Eliahu Goldratt (1999)

CARE, Mike Larkin and Diane Shea-Larkin (2000)

THE BETTER PEOPLE LEADER, Charles Coonradt (2007)

Workplace Champion Insights

People

Our Personal Assets are Knowledge, Attitude, Skills, and Habits (KASH)

Coaching Skills - Lead by asking questions and recognizing hidden skills

Interviewing Technique for Supervisors: Build cooperative goals and plans

Human Needs Analysis to Modify Behavior - Meet The Five Human Needs

Emotional Barriers - Psychological FEARs of failure, embarrassment, achievement, rejection

Use Left(IQ) and Right(EQ) Brain Thinking - Acquiring balance

Hiring by TASTE - Time control, positive Attitude, appropriate job Skills, Team spirit, Empathy

Schedule Regular Review Meetings - Scheduled 1:1s to communicate support and mutual trust

The Lizard Effect - Change requires growing a new skin of habits

Discipline: Coach for Success, Don't Police for Failure

Habit of Learning - Unskilled-Unaware > Unskilled-Aware>Aware-Skilled > Skilled-Unaware

{you} INC. - Personal Assets in 6 areas

Force Analysis - What's propelling you, what's holding you back

Skills plus Self-Image (belief) Mandate

Yours and Mine Roles & Responsibilities List

Management

Selling Skills-determine needs and wants of your buyer before offering the sale

Consensus Building - Obtain buy-in from all persons who will influence a decision

Negotiating Circles - Look for overlaps to build consensus

Behavior Style: decide/promote/support/analyze - behaviors that affect work performance

Progressive Applied Learning Model - Train/\Drain cycles averted

IDEAL Employee Exercise - Worst-IDEAL-Best Table

Employee Development Continuum and Leadership Model

The Power of Words - "Fascinating"(opportunity gate) vs "Frustrating"(barrier)

The Creativity of Opposites - Thinking the opposite of the obvious often reveals opportunities

Force Analysis: What's propelling you, what's holding you back?

Prioritize your tasks and goals on To-Do lists

Use the Timeline Tool (What's done, What's to come) to acknowledge achievements and set goals.

Employee Turnover Matrix

Decision-Making Matrix to Normalize Choices

Responsibility/Role Assessment - RACI: Who's Responsible, Accountable, Consulted, Informed

Run Effective Meetings (1:1s, Brainstorming, Planning, Projects, Teams, Informational)

Use Behavior Style Analysis to enhance compatibility and achievement and arm your teams

Personal

Use Simple Tools - Pen, Notebook, Desktop Calendar, To-Do Lists, Champion Logbooks

Time Control - Prioritizing activities to achieve goals, eliminating what need not be done

Goal-Setting - Short term sub-goals take you to the long-term goals in achievable steps

Throughput Analysis - Breaking through systemic log jams with cause and effect logic

Planning - to address Challenges, Opportunities, and Beneficiary needs

Team Development Steps - Creation Conflict Connection Collaboration Celebration

Four Phases of Turnover Costs - IN/hired and trained, WIN/productive and motivated, POUT/discontented, OUT/game over

Non-Productive/Productive Motivated/De-Motivated/Terminated Matrix **(CSQ)**

Recognition and Rewards build commitment

Quotes

It is better to allow the listener to interpret a subject's mood from your description of his actions.

Never say anything in private that you wouldn't say in public.

People don't do anything for the wrong reasons. They do it for the right reasons, in their own minds.

When speaking about another's performance, always talk as if that person is listening.

Trial and Error are slow and painful, but they are effective.

System shifting by workers occurs in companies where communication between workers and top management is weak.

Your success is based largely on how well you help others meet their needs by what you do.

Remember to always sell the actions you want another to take.

As you learn about the strengths of your workers, you are building trust with them.

This is your fundamental purpose: to serve your boss.

Using a positive word helps us refocus on a "problem"; thinking of it as a "challenge" instead. This refocusing guides our thoughts towards solutions, because the word "challenge" itself implies that there is a solution. Problems are barriers, challenges are opportunities.

Taking risks is how people grow.

MIND OVER MATTER: if you don't mind, it won't matter.

Show interest in them and they will show interest in you.

There's no sense in doing the wrong things very well.

Words have the power to steer your thoughts and emotions.

Empathy is the secret ingredient that enables a leader to negotiate agreements and build consensus.

Good time management is described as ensuring that what you are doing right now is moving you toward your personal or organizational goals.

Is what you are doing right now moving you toward the company's mission?

A good Mission Statement is a direction, not a destination.

A climbing turnover rate is deadly to a company.

Companies are known by the people they keep.

Workplace Champion: a fully trained and motivated, highly productive employee.

People are like lizards when it comes to change. They must shed their old habits and adopt new ones.

There is risk in change without proper preparation.

Random attention on what must be done each day is what wastes time.

Nothing grows in the soil of despair.

Negative thought is an unhealthy environment for positive results.

Workplace champions are all around you. Look for them, find them, and release their power.

Champion Rules

Adopt the paradigm of service towards everyone you meet.

Pay attention to what you want more of.

Recognize the good in people.

Learn the key to internal motivation and you will see continuous development.

Study and practice employee MOTIVATION

Link each task or project to an employee's internally-driven urge to satisfy their specific needs.

Training therefore should be self-motivated.

Start and end each meeting with a reference to a goal.

Training should be done in small applications over a longer period of time to allow time for the brain to assimilate and the body to practice the new knowledge.

Additional work assigned to your employees should be a challenge, but not a burden.

Encourage your employees to get involved in their own development. Training should be a positive response to their needs not a forced response to yours.

The more hooks you work into assignments, the stronger their motivation to do it well.

Union agreements are designed to protect both the employee and management from improper practices.

Make decisions that all stakeholders have confidence in and that are somehow justifiable.

Put a little something into the project for everyone and you will minimize any challenges or roadblocks.

In negotiation, learn the interests of each group and look for overlaps between their circles of interest.

Plan your projects to please the most people.

If you manage someone at work who behaves in a strange way, one way to resolve the problem is to consider which of the five basic human needs is being met by the behavior.

Champion Stories

Author's Note:

For more workplace championship strategies such as these, subscribe to my Workplace Champion blog site and receive regular articles on how to succeed as a workplace champion. **www.WorkplaceChampion.com**

Join us, receive a gift. John Smithman, Vancouver, Canada

John Smithman

John was born in Montreal on April 5 1942.

In 1962, after leaving Montreal's Concordia University, John wanted to become a commercial photographer. He took formal training at L'École Polytechnique de Photographie in Montréal. He joined the Canadian Airforce in 1962 to practice his new skill, but they had other ideas. He was given leadership training and taught to fly. He earned his 'pilot wings' in 1963 and flew with the Air Force until 1968 when he left to fly for Air Canada.

But, in 1970, John was lured away from Air Canada by a group of investors who wanted him to help them build their own airline in the Ottawa Valley near Pembroke, Ontario. On their behalf, John applied for a Class II Air Carrier license, bought an aircraft, rented a back up plane, hired and trained needed staff and pilots and began scheduled daily flights to Toronto. The company grew quickly and was still flying 20 years later.

In 1979, John moved to a warmer climate in Vancouver and took a job with The University of British Columbia where he headed up two service departments. There, he was responsible for significant operational changes and won International recognition for building design and creative management. He presented his new concepts to his peers at other universities across Canada. He sat on transportation boards representing The University and spearheaded reductions in multiple occupancy vehicles.

In 1996, John left UBC and founded Champions in the Workplace, a management training and coaching company, to teach his creative management concepts to other managers across Western Canada.

John finally got to practice photography in 2004 when he became the official photographer at Canada's largest magic club, The Vancouver Magic Circle. John still operates Champions in the Workplace where he offers coaching and consulting to managers and supervisors in Vancouver. Now 72, John is being pressured to retire, but before going he wanted to write a book on coaching supervisors. Better supervisors are critically needed at most organizations, but training is expensive and largely overlooked.

John's book Workplace Champion By Example makes his effective coaching skills available to others and offers his legacy to the workplace.